PRESERVATION
AND THE
MANAGEMENT
OF
LIBRARY
COLLECTIONS

PRESERVATION AND THE MANAGEMENT OF LIBRARY COLLECTIONS

by

John Feather

THE LIBRARY ASSOCIATION • LONDON

Published by
Library Association Publishing Ltd
7 Ridgmount Street
London WC1E 7AE

First published 1991

British Library Cataloguing in Publication Data

Feather, John
    Preservation and the management of library collections.
    1. Libraries. Stock. Conservation
    I. Title
    025.84

ISBN 0-85365-769-6

Typeset in 10/12pt Baskerville by Library Association Publishing Ltd
Printed and made in Great Britain by Billing & Sons Ltd, Worcester

Contents

Illustrations

Tables

Preface

Preservation has become one of the less predictable fashions in librarianship in the last decade of the twentieth century. Until comparatively recently, what was usually called 'conservation' was thought of as one of those esoteric matters which exercised the minds of archivists and rare book librarians, and was as remote as those specialists themselves from the concerns of other members of the profession. Suddenly, or so it seemed, conservation came out of the closet of the rare books room. It emerged under a new name – *preservation* – and with a new purpose. It was no longer merely a means of preserving the past for hypothetical readers in the indefinite future, but an essential part of the growing art of collection management, an art whose implementation was forced on so many libraries by the financial constraints to which they were subject. The need to take proper care of existing collections for the benefit of users seemed to grow in importance as the possibility of augmenting those collections diminished with each year's budgetary forecasts and book inflation statistics.

Preservation was argued to be relevant throughout the information professions. There was a growing perception of the problem of access to information in the many different formats which have been invented in the last century, and more particularly in the last twenty years. Was it possible to preserve digitized information at all? Or could digitization actually prove to be the solution to the problem of preserving information originally issued in print? Merely to ask these questions was to propose a new scope, purpose and significance for the most ancient of the librarian's arts, the art of custodianship.

The preservation of information in an accessible form is the subject of this book. It is not a book about bookbinding or paper repair. It is a book about professional librarianship and library management, and it is intended for those whose professional concern is (or will be) with the effective management of the information resource which lies at the heart of every information agency. Whether that resource is a stock of books, or a collection of historical documents, or the discs and tapes of a database is irrelevant. Without access to information in a retrievable form, an information agency has no purpose, and so ultimately, somewhere, that information must be held in a format which has a physical existence. The survival of the information is therefore dependent upon the survival of the medium in which it is held. The preservation of information is therefore a central professional issue, and it is thus that it is presented here.

At the core of this book is a consideration of how a preservation policy is developed and managed, but technical matters cannot be ignored. If all our information-carrying media were permanent and incorruptible, there would be no preservation problem. But they are not, and they never can be. All of them are physical objects with a chemical constitution. None of them is entirely inert or stable. An understanding of the basic scientific facts of information storage systems is essential to an understanding of how to preserve the information itself. Such matters as the chemistry of paper or the reaction of photographic film to sunlight need not concern us in detail, but those who seek to preserve information held in those formats need to know enough about them to ensure that they are stored and used in a way which is indeed consistent with their continued existence.

There is no necessary conflict between preservation and access. Our professional business is to transfer information from where it is held to where it is needed. That is facilitated, not inhibited, by the proper storage of the information itself. Therein lies the theme and the message of this book.

Acknowledgements

My own students in the Department of Library and Information Studies at Loughborough University have made a greater contribution to this book than they may realize. Those who have taken the courses on the preservation of library materials and on collection management in the last few years will recognize some of the materials and ideas in this book. To some extent they have been the unwitting guinea-pigs for an attempt to evolve an approach to presenting the subject which is appropriate to its place among the professional concerns of the 1990s. I am grateful to them for their tolerance.

More broadly, I have been fortunate enough to discuss preservation with many of those most intimately involved in it, both in the United Kingdom and overseas. None of them can be held responsible for what is here, and some may even disagree with a few of my ideas. Nevertheless, Jean-Marie Arnoult, Terry Belanger, David Clements, Josephine Fang, Graham Matthews, Fred Ratcliffe, Merrily Smith and Michael Turner have all, in their various ways, influenced my thinking on the subject.

My former secretary, Cynthia Robinson, coped with both me and my handwriting. Only those who know the latter will understand the enormity of that achievement.

Once again, I have written a book which is not dedicated to my wife. No such act, however symbolic, could ever repay all that I owe to her.

John Feather
Loughborough University

1   *Preservation: a problem defined*

The central task of the librarian is to make information available to users. To achieve this he or she has to organize, both physically and intellectually, the media which contain information. This, however, is a futile operation if either the documents themselves, or the information which they contain, are not available for consultation. The information, the *raison d'être* of the document, will indeed be lost if the media which carry it are not preserved in a usable form. This latter truth has been somewhat eclipsed in recent years, but it remains true. The development of new media of information storage to supplement the traditional written or printed documents has been a significant element in the growth of this neglect. The new storage media are, for the most part, comparatively easy to replicate so that their physical preservation seems of little importance. Much of the information for which such media are used is, in any case, considered by its originators to be of comparatively short-term interest, since it can so easily be updated. For both of these reasons, preservation has seemed to be unnecessary. Moreover, modern librarianship rightly emphasizes service to users rather than the mere accumulation of materials as the primary professional concern. Instant access to information is regarded as the ideal – at least by information providers – and there is an implicit assumption that what is needed is the 'new' or up-to-date information which is most likely to be contained in the most recent publications, whatever their physical form. Preservation of materials is too easily dismissed as the esoteric concern of the archivist or the rare book librarian, of little or no interest even in the mainstream of academic or public librarianship, let alone in the fashionable electronic world of information science.

The fundamental fallacy in this line of argument will be explored later, but we must begin by considering the concept of 'preservation' and defining some of the words which we shall be using. Three terms need to be clearly understood, and the distinction between them carefully maintained. These are:

1

- preservation
- conservation
- restoration

Preservation is an aspect of the management of the library. Its objective is to ensure that information survives in a usable form for as long as it is wanted. In many cases, this implies the survival for the same period of time of the physical medium which contains that information, whether it is a manuscript, a printed book, a videotape or a floppy disk. In most cases, the medium will be that in which the information was originally stored and disseminated by its originator or publisher, although this is not a necessary condition for the preservation of the information. Indeed, the preservation of the original medium is sometimes undesirable and occasionally impossible. The essential characteristic of preservation is that it is a large-scale operation, concerned with the effective management of the library's stock, or information resource.

Conservation is one aspect of preservation activity. It normally implies the active use of preventative measures, or processes of repair of damaged material, to ensure the continued existence of individual items. Even here, however, there is an important managerial element. The decision on intervention – that is, the decision to repair a particular item – is essentially managerial or professional. The decision on the process and materials to be used may be technical, but even that has to be taken within the broad parameters of managerially determined policy, and, in the case of materials of historical importance, professional guidance and judgment are essential.

Restoration is the least common and the least useful of the three terms, for in this context it has a very precise meaning. It is taken to mean the attempt to restore a damaged item to its original condition by careful imitation of materials and techniques. Such an activity can, of course, be justified in aesthetic and historical terms. We do not repair medieval cathedrals with reinforced concrete (or at least not in their visible parts); it would be equally insensitive to restore a medieval manuscript with a binding covered in imitation leather. In practice, the cost of restoration, and the use of the rare skills which it demands, can be justified only in a very few cases of books of outstanding beauty or importance, whose significance as museum objects is at least as great as their significance as carriers of information.

It has become conventional to regard the Florence flood of 1966 as the beginning of the recent revival of interest in the preservation of books and documents. In the autumn of that year, the River Arno burst its banks in the middle of the city and caused devastating damage. Among the flooded buildings was the Biblioteca Nazionale, where nearly half a million books and manuscripts suffered from the inflow of water and mud. A huge international rescue effort was mounted by Unesco, with binders and conservators who were recruited from all over the world to help in restoring the library's treasures. The sheer size of the problem which confronted them forced them to develop new techniques for dealing with water-damaged paper and bookbindings. Some of these techniques, especially that of freeze-drying, have now become standard practice throughout the world. Moreover, since there were not enough trained personnel to cope with the work, a whole generation of conservators had to be trained at Florence, or were trained subsequently by those who learned their craft there. Florence was indeed a critical episode in the history of conservation and restoration. Old skills which might otherwise have been lost were handed on to a new generation, while the new techniques have proved invaluable elsewhere. In one sense, however, the response to the disaster at the Biblioteca Nazionale had a negative effect, for, in some eyes, it tended to confirm the traditional image of conservation: as a matter for those concerned with rare books and manuscripts, and, moreover, as a craft-based activity dealing with individual books and documents whose practitioners were skilled, meticulous and inordinately slow.[1]

The real impetus for the modern preservation movement came not only from Italy but also from the United States, from the Library of Congress as well as the Biblioteca Nazionale. The Library of Congress, although it has great collections of earlier material, is primarily a library of nineteenth- and twentieth-century books. The legal deposit collections which form the largest single group of its holdings are, by definition, from the period since the Library was founded in 1800, and most of them indeed date from after the 1840s. Consequently, a very high proportion of the books in the Library of Congress's collection are printed on paper dating from the worst period in the history of papermaking. To exacerbate matters, throughout the nineteenth century American paper (on which, of course, by far the largest part of the Library of Congress's holdings are printed) was even worse than its European equivalent. Other American research libraries are in the same position; the New York Public Library, in particular, has vast and important nineteenth- and twentieth-century holdings.

The basic problem which the libraries confronted was a simple physical one: the decaying acidic paper had become embrittled, and could no longer be handled. Any pressure caused it to disintegrate, and even on the shelves the paper was quietly deteriorating without any handling at all. The problem of brittle paper, and its chemical causes, had been understood since the early years of the century.[2] By the 1930s, it was a matter of concern to both British and American librarians.[3] In the same decade, the New York Public Library recognized the implications of the problem, and initiated a major programme to make microfilms of endangered books.[4] However, the full extent of the problem was not appreciated until the 1960s, when its scale was revealed in a series of surveys of major American libraries. The situation was at its worst in the industrial cities of the north-east and mid-west of the United States, but it was not good anywhere. At Columbia University in New York City it was estimated in 1975 that some 30% of the library's holdings of about five million items were embrittled;[5] the corresponding figure at Berkeley, in the comparatively unpolluted atmosphere of the San Francisco Bay area, was 10%.[6] It was, however, at the Library of Congress and New York Public Library that the position was worst. In the mid-1970s it was calculated that some six million of the former's seventeen million books were in an *advanced* stage of deterioration. At the New York Public, with its research collections housed in an ageing building in mid-town Manhattan, the figure was as high as 50%. It was suggested that in both libraries, all of the non-fiction published between 1900 and 1939 would be unusable by the end of the century.[7] This was the *real* preservation crisis, far greater in extent, if less likely to grab the headlines in the world's newspapers, than any damage caused by the Arno in Florence.

It was clear that a problem on this scale required solutions which were quite different in degree and in kind from the traditional techniques of the craftsman conservator. Even the new methods developed in Florence, and indeed the new workers trained there, could not cope with the crisis gradually revealed in the late 1960s and early 1970s. The traditional conservators were essentially trained to deal with books printed or written on handmade papers, and bound by hand using traditional methods and materials. Such work was as time-consuming as it was skilful and could only be used for a tiny number of books. Temporary measures could indeed be used to prevent the further deterioration of damaged books, but such solutions as boxing could not cope with the millions of decaying items in the major American libraries.

Even if a mass boxing programme could be funded and undertaken, the books would continue to decay inside the boxes. This was a problem which was fundamentally different from that of the typical seventeenth- or eighteenth-century book, where the conservator was normally confronted with a broken-down binding but paper which was essentially sound. What was now at stake was the text-block itself, and therefore the print which it contained. It was nineteenth- and twentieth-century materials, rather than those from earlier periods, which were now the centre of concern.

This called for a fundamental shift of emphasis in the planning and implementation of preservation programmes, a shift which took two directions:

- the scale and speed of the techniques used had to be appropriate to the size of the problem and the rapidity of its development;
- the text and the information which it contained rather than the book itself became the principal objective of preservation.

The sheer size of the problem of acidic and embrittled paper, especially in the United States, called for the development of mass techniques which were not only different from those used by craftsman conservators but which were derived from a fundamentally different philosophy. The meticulous treatment of individual items could no longer be seen as the salvation of the millions of books and documents which were now recognized to be in imminent danger not merely of damage but of total destruction. For those which had not yet disintegrated there was some possibility of rescue if the acidity which was the cause of their problems could be removed from the paper, or if its effects could be neutralized. A great deal of time and money was devoted to research into the deacidification of paper by the Library of Congress, the Council on Library Resources and other agencies in the United States and elsewhere.

The results have been encouraging. A number of deacidification processes have been developed. Some seem to be successful in treating large numbers of books simultaneously. The capital costs are high, because the processes are designed to operate on a large scale, and therefore have to be carried out in industrial-sized plants if they are to be cost-effective. A number of such plants have been built or are in the course of construction, using several different techniques. The size and cost inevitably mean that they are enterprises at a national or regional level, with large infusions of public funding. National

5

libraries dominate the move towards mass deacidification, since they alone can justify the costs and gain access to the funding. The *methyl magnesium carbonate system* installed by the Bibliothèque nationale at its Centre de conservation at Sablé can treat some 4,000 books per week.[8] The *Wei T'o nonaqueous book deacidification system* developed by the Public Archives of Canada is now used to treat some 40,000 items per year at that country's National Library.[9] The Library of Congress, coping with a problem on an unparalleled scale, intends to respond accordingly. Its *diethyl zinc process* (DEZ) facility may be opened in 1990, and will have the capacity to treat one million volumes annually.[10] Not all of these have been equally successful. The first DEZ plant was destroyed by an explosion in 1986, and it has been argued that the process is scientifically unproven.[10] Deacidification, however, cannot be expected to rescue all of the endangered books in all the libraries of the world, and it does nothing to solve the problem presented by those which are already beyond rescue.

The preservation of the information content of a book or document, as opposed to the original physical format, is sometimes the only solution to preserving it at all. In practice, this means the creation of so-called 'surrogates', in which the information is recorded in another medium, but in its original visual form. This is most readily achieved by photography, and in practice the normal surrogate medium is microform, usually 35-mm roll film. Preservation microfilming has been undertaken since the 1930s, when it was pioneered at the New York Public Library. Indeed it marked the beginning of that institution's response to its recognition of its massive preservation problem. It has subsequently become a widespread practice, and is now the normal means of ensuring the availability of long runs of newspapers and journals, as well as the contents of decaying books. In the United States, although not in Europe, it is not uncommon for the original to be abandoned once the master negative has been made, so that the film becomes the only source of the data.[11]

Electronic storage systems are theoretically very attractive as surrogates instead of, or in addition to, film.[12] Digitization still presents economic and technical problems, but the technology of the optical disk seems to have considerable potential for preservation. It can record both the information content and the visual appearance of the text in the original book or document, just like a film, and the retrieval methods are, of course, far more powerful. At present, however, there is still a serious problem with the medium of the optical disk, for its own long-term survival properties have not yet been fully established. Photographic film, on the other hand, if it is properly processed and stored, will survive for longer than most acidic papers – up to 500 years – and can thus be argued to have precisely the archival qualities which are required for preservation purposes. There is a further consequence of the rapid development of new electronic storage media. The rapid supercession of one system by another is hardly the ideal circumstance in which to create surrogates designed for permanent preservation. A number of electronic media are already obsolete, and the equipment on which to run them is no longer generally available. Photographic film formats, on the other hand, are standardized throughout the world, and although the projection or viewing equipment may be modernized, the basic capacity to view 35-mm roll film or 105-mm microfiche remains constant.[13]

Mass deacidification and mass surrogacy programmes have been two of the most potent and effective responses to the preservation crisis, and in particular to the problems posed by the embrittlement of acidic paper. Both are in origin American solutions to what was first seen as an American problem, although both have been applied successfully in Europe and indeed elsewhere in the world. Neither, however, is a total solution to the preservation problem, and their advocates would not, indeed, make such a claim. The issue has a far wider dimension; in particular there is a growing acceptance of the need to take preventative measures which will ensure that the present crisis will not recur in the future, or at least will have the effect of reducing it to a manageable size.

Perhaps the most important single development in the preservation field in the last twenty years has been the recognition of the universality of the problem. Decaying newspapers, perhaps unique, are as likely to be found in the local studies section of a public library as they are in some great national repository. All libraries have a problem if the majority of the books and journals that they buy have a built-in obsolescence of little more than two or three decades, and if their structure is so poor that the binding will not survive even two years of normal use. Rising prices and falling budgets have forced librarians to reconsider the rate of redundancy and replacement of stock, while the continuous growth of the publishing industry places ever increasing demands on those same diminishing budgets. More books and less money means that those books which are selected have to be chosen more carefully before they are bought, and cherished more effectively after they have been acquired. The selection and management of the stock has become a live issue in librarianship during the last decade of economic stringency to a far greater extent than it ever was during the expansive decades after World War II.

The economic aspect problem is perhaps at its most acute in the United Kingdom, where public funding of libraries is most widespread. Britain's vast network of public libraries, unparalleled anywhere in the world, is entirely dependent upon the vagaries of central and local government policy for its budget. Moreover, in Britain, unlike the United States, virtually the entire academic library system is also publicly funded, either directly or indirectly. The continuous financial pressure on public sector budgets since 1979 has inevitably meant that almost all public and academic libraries have suffered severe *de facto* cuts in their budgets, since the increases in book funds have never kept pace with the rate of price inflation. Stocks and indeed services have suffered, and the need to preserve stock has become ever more obvious, especially as the quality of service provision tends to be specially protected. It is against this background that we have to consider the British approach to preservation, which has been distinctively different from that of the Americans; naturally enough, it reflects circumstances in the United Kingdom just as the American approach reflects those in the United States.

During the late 1970s, the British Library gradually came to recognize the extent of its own conservation problem. In its first annual report, in 1974, the British Library Board announced that it was 'deeply concerned about the problem of conservation',[14] a sentiment which it repeated ('great concern'[15]) in the following year. In 1975 a Conservation Branch was established, which during the next five years developed an active, but conventional, policy for the care of the stock. Substantial funds were made available for conservation, but they seem to have been devoted largely to the repair of individual items. A survey of the collections, however, revealed that the British Library's problem, although different from that of the Library of Congress, was in some ways just as great. Two centuries of neglect, not always very benign, had left some of the collections in a parlous condition. A century of storage in overcrowded and badly ventilated bookstacks in the heart of a polluted city had not helped. Finally, three decades of vastly increased use since 1945 had completed the process of creating the perfect circumstances for large-scale and serious damage. As a consequence, resources had to be redirected. In 1979 – 80, expenditure on conservation exceeded that on acquisitions for the first time, and by the early 1980s, the Conservation Branch was involved in a 'sustained campaign for the care of books among staff and readers',[16] in the creation of microform surrogates, and in research on deacidification. By the late 1980s, a further survey had revealed that some 14% of the Library's post-1850 books were on embrittled paper, yet again emphasizing the sheer scale of the problem.[17] In 1988 – 9, the Humanities and Social Sciences Division (the former Reference Division) spent nearly £5.5 million on preservation.[18]

However, even the neutral prose of the Board's annual reports cannot conceal a distinct change in philosophy in the early 1980s. In 1983 – 4, the *Conservation Branch* was replaced by a *Preservation Service*,[19] and began to put ever more emphasis on mass preservation, especially microform surrogate programmes. Cheaper processes of boxing and rebinding, and what the report for 1986 – 7 rather coyly called 'greater emphasis on lower-cost options',[20] became the main thrust of the Library's policy, while it also began to play a more active role in the identification and partial solution of preservation problems on a national scale.

During the same ten or fifteen years, the other national libraries of the United Kingdom made equally alarming discoveries about the state of their stocks and the cost of remedying the problems. The National Library of Scotland estimated in 1986 that 15 – 20% of its stock was in need of active intervention if it was to be preserved. A budget of £600,000 per year had been allocated, but the Library's preservation manager was far from complacent about the level of activity.[21] Two years later, the budget had not increased.[22] The situation in Wales is comparable; preservation activity has increased at the National Library but, as elsewhere, cannot match the scale of the problem.[23]

It is against this background that the Ratcliffe Report,[24] for which the research was funded by the British Library, has to be seen. This document, published in 1984, can now be seen as a turning-point in the definition and understanding of library preservation in the United Kingdom. Its methodology, and hence its findings, reflect the preoccupations of British librarians, and especially those of the senior managers of the Reference Division of the British Library, in the early 1980s. It was essentially a survey of attitudes and opinions, and it revealed alarming ignorance and perhaps equally alarming naïvety about the preservation issue itself and the solutions which were available. An astonishing 162 out of 332 libraries which responded to a questionnaire (about 80% of those circulated) declared their intention to retain between

81 and 100% of their stock 'permanently'. Yet only 9 libraries actually had a written preservation policy statement. Staff training in conservation was minimal everywhere and non-existent in 189 libraries. The subject had all but vanished from the curricula of library schools, and only 36 libraries offered even the most basic preservation awareness training to their staff.[25] The gap between intention and practice suggested that few British library managers had given any real thought to the implications of their traditional policies of permanent retention of the entire stock. This was, perhaps, especially true in the university sector, and in the major urban public libraries. Ratcliffe's findings were to exercise a seminal influence on developments for the rest of the 1980s.

The need for training and education to remedy the general ignorance of the preservation issue was one of Ratcliffe's principal recommendations. There is some evidence that this has already had some effect. In particular, there has been an emphasis on in-service training for practitioners, on the teaching of preservation management in library schools to new entrants to the profession, and on the inclusion of preservation awareness in induction courses for non-professional staff and in user education programmes. Quite apart from the important developments in the library schools,[26] academic libraries in particular have responded to the situation which Ratcliffe revealed. By 1986 there was already a slight improvement, if only in the sense that nearly 50% of librarians claimed to have been influenced by Ratcliffe's findings.[27] In 1988 it was found that 17 out of 53 member libraries of SCONUL (a 76% response) had a written preservation policy (compared with Ratcliffe's finding of 2), and the number of full-time and presumably expert conservation officers had doubled from 12 to 24. Nine additional institutions (to Ratcliffe's 20) had systematically conducted preservation surveys of their stock, and 19 (as against 2) had prepared a disaster plan.[28] At this level, therefore, it is clear that some British academic libraries responded rapidly and positively to the preservation crisis once it was identified. If public libraries have been less immediately responsive, it is at least partly because they have so many other calls on even more limited funds and staff. In some quarters, there is at least enthusiasm, knowledge and commitment.[29]

The large and growing descriptive literature on preservation in libraries of all kinds gives valuable insights into the problem as it is perceived by practitioners. Of course, every library has its own unique problems, but the recurrence of certain themes in the literature suggests that there are also some areas of shared interest, even between apparently very disparate institutions. The physical causes of the preservation problem are common to all libraries, archives and information agencies. Information cannot exist in a permanent form unless it is stored in some medium. All the information media have a physical base, whether it is paper or vinyl or celluloid. If the physical base is lost then the information held on it is also lost. That is the fundamental issue of preservation: to transmit the message, we have to preserve the medium.

That objective must, of course, be seen in a wider context. The same physical faults which are the root cause of the preservation problem make it impossible, even if it were desirable, to preserve everything everywhere. Archivists have always recognized the need for selectivity. They accept the unpalatable truth that 'some records will have to be left to decay',[30] and a similar attitude will have to be developed by librarians, even by those who see themselves primarily as custodians of the heritage. To preserve information, it may even be necessary to sacrifice the original medium. The complex and expensive techniques of restoration can never be justified for more than a tiny minority of books and manuscripts.[31] The essence of the matter is, therefore, selectivity. Selection, however, would be pointless if it were random. It is therefore necessary to have criteria to help to determine the priority of each case. To develop a policy which will define those criteria it is necessary to understand the physical facts which make the policy necessary in the first place. For that reason, a librarian needs to know something of the physical basis of books and other media.

Nevertheless, a knowledge of the chemistry of paper or the technique of case-binding is not to be confused with an understanding of preservation. In the last analysis, preservation policy consists of a series of decisions determined by considerations of organization and finance as well as by the use and contents of the library. Preservation is expensive. If it is to be more than the temporary repair of randomly selected items, an informed and agreed policy is needed. The preservation problem has a physical cause, but its solution can only come from good, effective and well-informed management.

References

1   Ogden, S., 'The impact of the Florence flood on library conservation in the United States of America', *Restaurator*, **3**, 1979, 1 – 36; and Waters, P., 'The Florence flood of 1966 revisited', in Palmer, R. E. (ed.), *Preserving the word* (Library Association Conference Proceedings, Harrogate, 1986), London, The Library Association, 1987, 113 – 28.

2 Among the early scientific literature is Irvine, R. and Woodhead, G. S., 'On the presence in paper of residual chemicals used in its preparation', *Journal of the Society of the Chemical Industry*, **13**, 1894, 131 – 33. Early library literature includes Johnson, R., 'Inferior paper', *Library journal*, **16**, 1891, 241 – 42.

3 See, for example, The Library Association, *The durability of paper*, London, The Library Association, 1930; and Jarrell, T. D. (ed.), *Deterioration of book and record papers*, Washington, D C, Department of Agriculture, 1936.

4 Bourke, T. A., 'The New York Public Library Register of Microform Masters', *Microform review*, **13**, 1984 – 5, 17 – 21.

5 Battin, P., 'Preservation at the Columbia University libraries', in Merrill-Oldham, J., and Smith, M. (eds.), *The Library Preservation Program. Models, priorities, possibilities*, Chicago, Ill., American Library Association 1985, 34.

6 Ogden, B. W., 'Determining conservation options at the University of California at Berkeley', in Merrill-Oldham and Smith, *The Library Preservation Program*, 64 – 5.

7 Library of Congress, Preservation Office, *A national preservation program. Proceedings of a planning conference*, Washington, D C, Library of Congress, 1980, 14.

8 Arnoult, J.-M., 'Mass deacidification at the Bibliothèque nationale', in Smith, M. A. (ed.), *Preservation of library materials* (Conference held at the National Library of Austria, Vienna, 7 – 19 April 1986, sponsored by the Conference of Directors of National Libraries in co-operation with IFLA and Unesco), 2 vols, Munich, London, New York, Paris, K. G. Saur (IFLA Publications, 40, 41), 1987, vol. 2, 129 – 33.

9 Scott, M., 'Mass deacidification at the National Library of Canada', in Smith, *Preservation of library materials*, vol. 2, 134 – 6.

10 Sparks, P. G., 'Mass deacidification at the Library of Congress', in Smith, *Preservation of library materials*, vol. 2, 137 – 40; and Thompson, J. C., 'Mass deacidification: thoughts on the Cunha Report', *Restaurator*, **9**, 1988, 147 – 62.

11 Walker, G., 'Preserving the intellectual content of deteriorated library materials', in Morrow, C. C. (ed.), *The preservation challenge. A guide to conserving library materials*, White Plains, NY, Knowledge Industry Publications, 1983, 93 – 113; and Gwinn, N. E. (ed.), *Preservation microfilming. A guide for librarians and archivists*, Chicago, Ill., London, American Library Association, 1987.

12 Lynch, C. A. and Brownrigg, E. B.,'Conservation, preservation and digitization', *College and research libraries*, **47**, 1986, 379 – 84; and Cannon, T., 'A review of the new technologies', in National Preservation Office, *Preservation and technology* (National Preservation Office Seminar Papers, 3), London, The British Library, 1989, 47 – 52.

13 Meadows, A. J., 'The medium and the message', in National Preservation Office, *Preservation and technology*, 1 – 9.

14 The British Library, *First annual report*, London, The British Library, 1974, 5.

15 The British Library, *Annual report 1974 – 75*, London, The British Library, 1975, 6.

16 The British Library, *Annual report 1980 – 81*, London, The British Library, 1981, 25.

17 Pollock, M., 'Surveying the collections', *Library conservation news*, **21**, October 1988, 4 – 6.

18 The British Library, *Annual report 1988 – 89*, London, The British Library, 1989, 53.

19 The British Library, *Annual report 1983 – 84*, London, The British Library, 1984, 9.

20 The British Library, *Annual report 1986 – 87*, London, The British Library, 1987, 26.

21 Hutton, B. G., 'Preservation policy at the National Library of Scotland', in Palmer, *Preserving the word*, 26 – 8.

22 Hutton, B. G., 'Preserving Scotland's heritage', *Library conservation news*, **19**, April 1988, 1 – 3.

23 Rees, E., 'Wales and the preservation problem', in Palmer, *Preserving the word*, 29 – 32; and Rees, E., 'Wales and the preservation problem', *Library conservation news*, **18**, January 1988, 1 – 3.

24 Ratcliffe, F. W., *Preservation policies and conservation in British libraries: Report of the Cambridge University Library Conservation Project*, London, The British Library (Library and Information Research Report, 25), 1984. See also below, 99 – 100.

25 Ratcliffe, *Preservation policies*, 16 – 30.

26 Feather, J. and Lusher, A., 'Education for conservation in British library schools: current practices and future prospects', *Journal of librarianship*, **21**, 1989, 129 – 38.

27 Mowat, I. R. M., 'Preservation problems in academic libraries', in Palmer, *Preserving the word*, 38.

28 Moon, B. E. and Loveday, A. J., 'Progress report on preservation in universities since the Ratcliffe Report', in National Preservation Office, *Preservation and technology*, 11 – 17.

29 Beard, J. C., 'Preservation problems in public libraries', in Palmer, *Preserving the word*, 46 – 50.

30 Thomas, D., 'Conservation: new techniques and new attitudes', *Archives*, **16**, 1983, 177.

31 For a very traditional approach, see Dachs, K., 'Conservation: the curator's point of view', *Restaurator*, **6**, 1984, 118 – 26.

2 *The materials of information storage*

Preservation has vast financial and organizational implications, which will be explored in Chapters 4, 5 and 6. However, as we have seen, there would be no problem if the materials on which we store information were not subject to damage and decay. Damage, whether by human agency or by other means, can be avoided to some extent, and certainly provisions can be made to minimize its consequences if it should happen by accident. Decay, however, is intrinsic to all the materials currently used for information storage. To understand the need for preservation, and the methods by which it can be achieved, it is therefore necessary to begin with an understanding of the nature of information storage materials, and the defects which are inherent to them.

Book materials

Paper

Paper is still the most common medium on which information is recorded. It has been so since before the invention of printing, and most of what has been stored in written or printed form is available only on paper. Some knowledge of the history and properties of paper is, therefore, the necessary starting-point in the study of preservation.

The Chinese invented paper in the fifth century AD; it gradually made its way westwards during the next three hundred years following the ancient trade routes of central Asia. The use of paper, and the knowledge of the papermaking process, reached the Middle East at about the time of the great Arab conquests of the seventh and eighth centuries. It was through the Arab incursions across the Mediterranean that paper and papermaking first reached southern Europe, in Sicily, Spain and Italy. By the thirteenth century it was in widespread use, to the extent that when printing was invented in the middle of the fifteenth century, paper was being manufactured in considerable quantities throughout southern and western Europe. The materials which it displaced – parchment and vellum – continued in use for some time, but paper had become the normal medium for written documents by the middle of the sixteenth century at the latest, and printed books were rarely produced on anything else.[1]

The basic constituent of paper is fibrous vegetable matter. This need not be taken directly from the plant, since vegetable fibres which have already been processed and manufactured can be recycled for use in papermaking. Indeed, paper itself can be used in this way, and frequently is; cheaper papers are almost invariably made by recycling used paper of a higher quality. Recycling has become even more common in recent years, with our growing concern about the rate at which we are consuming our natural resources. The fibres can also, however, be taken from other products, such as natural fabrics, especially linen and cotton cloth. The quality of the paper ultimately depends upon the quality of the vegetable matter from which it is made, and the manner in which it is processed when first used to make the paper and when reused.[2]

The original method of papermaking invented by the Chinese was an entirely hand-craft process. Essentially the same hand processes continued to be used in the west until the beginning of the nineteenth century, for the method never significantly changed. Indeed, even today some paper is still made by traditional hand methods, as a hobby in the west and for commercial papers (although not for ordinary printing) in some south-east Asian countries.[3] In the process of hand papermaking the first stage is to break down the vegetable matter, in whatever form, into its constituent fibres. This process was partially mechanized in the seventeenth century when a machine called a 'Hollander' was designed in which the material was beaten into pulp by hammers under a steady flow of water. The result of this process is a thick liquid pulp, known to papermakers as 'stuff', to which various other substances may then be added. These additives include a size which will seal the surface of the paper, for otherwise all paper would be absorbent like blotting paper; dyes, if coloured paper is being made; or bleach, if the fibres and the water being used will not give the paper a sufficiently 'white' appearance.

The stuff is picked out of the vat in which it has been made by means of a rectangular wooden frame called a 'mould' (see Figure 1). The longer side of the mould can be comfortably held in the hands of a man with his arms outstretched. Lengths of wire, at intervals of approximately

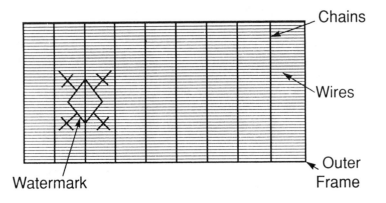

Fig. 1 The mould

two centimetres, run parallel to the shorter sides along the whole length of the mould. Parallel to the longer sides, and at much closer intervals (ideally of about one millimetre) run much thinner wires. The former are called *chains* and the latter *wires*. Sewn into them may be a pattern of wires which forms the papermaker's trade mark; this is called the 'watermark'. The papermaker also has a second, slightly larger, wooden frame called the 'deckle', with no chains or wires. The deckle fits snugly over the mould but has slightly protruding edges. When the papermaker dips the mould into the vat he picks up enough stuff to spread across the porous surface formed by the chains and wires. He shakes off any surplus water, and then puts the deckle onto the mould before shaking it again. Finally, he removes the deckle and turns out the sheet of wet, but now solidifying, stuff onto a sheet of felt. The felt absorbs the excess moisture, and the stuff dries into a sheet of paper. Another piece of felt is immediately placed on top of the sheet, and then the next sheet from the mould on top of that, and so on, until a pile of several hundred sheets of paper and felt has been formed. This is pressed to squeeze out any water which still remains. When the paper has lost all its moisture, the felt is removed and the drying process is then complete.

It is the chains, wires and watermark which enable us to identify paper made by this method. Where the stuff lies over them in the mould, the sheet is slightly thinner than it is elsewhere. Consequently, 'chain-lines' are formed where the paper is also a little thinner. If a sheet of hand-made paper is held up to the light, the chain-lines are clearly visible, as is the watermark. Although some modern machine-made

16

papers have artificial watermarks, few which are likely to be found in libraries or archives have artificial chain-lines. Chain-lines are consequently a very reliable indicator that the paper is hand-made.

Some understanding of this process is important because of its consequences for the preservation of the paper found in books and documents. The vegetable matter and the additives are critical to the strength and durability of the paper. Until the end of the eighteenth century, most western papers were made from linen rags. Such paper was of a very high quality, with a good general appearance and, most importantly, a high tensile strength. The stuff needed little by way of chemical additives to prepare it for use, and the paper itself was suitable for both writing and printing. It had to be sized so that ink would adhere to the surface, but little more was done to it. By the late eighteenth century, however, there was a serious problem. The demand for paper was increasing, both for printing and for other purposes. At the same time, the supply of linen rags was diminishing, as cotton replaced it as the cheapest fabric. Although cotton rags could be used for papermaking, they produced poor paper. To compensate for lower-quality materials papermakers began to use chlorine bleaches and other additives to provide the colour and strength which their customers demanded. In itself, this was only a temporary solution; in the end, the papermakers had to find new methods and new materials to satisfy the insatiable demand for their product. Thus began a decline in the quality of paper which was not to be arrested for more than a century.[4]

One of the long-term solutions to the problem of increased demand lay in the invention of a new method of papermaking, since the traditional method of hand manufacture was now too slow to be adequate. The papermaking machine was invented by a Frenchman, Nicolas-Louis Robert, in 1796. In those unpropitious times, he could find no backers in his own country, and so took himself and his designs to England. There he attracted the attention of the brothers Henry and Sealy Fourdrinier, who owned a wholesale stationery business in London. In 1806, with their financial support, the first working machine was built; it was named after its patrons rather than its inventor.

The basic principle upon which the Fourdrinier machine depended continues to be used in its modern successors. Fibres are pushed into the machine, and the stuff mechanically beaten, at one end (the 'wet' end). The stuff then flows from the vat onto a conveyor belt, where it is thinned to paper thickness, and dried out, either naturally or by jets of hot air. It emerges at the other end (the 'dry' end) as a continuous roll ('web') of paper which can be cut to the desired length, or divided into single sheets. The process is simple and effective, but it requires a much greater use of chemicals than does hand papermaking, as well as artificial drying mechanisms. The machines produced paper which was acceptable to its immediate users but whose long-term survival properties were significantly less than those of its hand-made, and largely unadulterated, predecessor.[5]

In the long term, the changes in the technology of papermaking were to be of lesser significance for preservation than were the changes in the paper's constituent materials. Throughout the nineteenth century, there was a search for new, and preferably cheaper, substances which would be easily available to papermakers as a substitute for the decreasing supply of increasingly expensive rags. For the first time, paper was made of raw vegetable matter which had not previously been subject to a manufacturing process. Various reeds and grasses were used experimentally in the 1840s and 1850s, but the final solution, and one which is still in use today, was the use of wood. Pulp made from wood fulfilled all the basic requirements of the nineteenth-century papermakers in terms of its cost and availability. In northern Europe and North America there were apparently unlimited quantities of it in the great forests, which were still largely unexploited. Two methods of pulping were invented; both are still in use. The first produces *mechanical wood* paper, by simply tearing apart the whole of the log, after the bark has been stripped away, and using water to convert it into pulp. This produces the very cheap but not particularly durable paper which is used, for example, for newspapers and paperbacks. The second process produces *chemical wood* paper. In this method, chemicals are used to catalyse changes in the molecular structure of the pulp. The effect is to produce a 'whiter' and visually more attractive paper of the sort used for writing and bookprinting. Chemical wood paper is also more durable than mechanical wood paper, although it is far from perfect when compared with good linen-rag papers.[6] However, the process of turning trees into paper is quick, cheap and simple. The paper which was thus created in the nineteenth century, was, destined to be a major cause of one of the most important aspects of the preservation crisis in the libraries of the world a century later.

The fundamental problem is that wood-based paper, whether mechanical or chemical, is naturally high in acidity. The lignin, one of its chemical constituents, oxidizes when it is in contact with the air; other chemicals which are present react badly to the ultraviolet spectrum of sunlight. The details need not detain us, but the consequences are crucial. In general terms, it is accurate to say that paper with a high acid content will decay naturally and irreversibly over a comparatively short period of time. For over a century, from the 1860s onwards, the great majority of European and American books were printed on acidic paper. Acidic paper was used for written (and later typewritten) documents. Bookbinders used it as a matter of course for endpapers and labels. Because the problem was not generally understood, no steps were taken to prevent or circumvent it until the 1970s, so that the most basic material of information storage and preservation was inherently unstable without the majority of its custodians even being aware of the fact.[7]

The scientific study of paper began in the late nineteenth century, but it was not until the 1930s that standards for permanent paper were first considered.[8] It was, of course, at the same time that the problem of embrittlement, which is the most significant manifestation of the chemical decay of paper, was being identified in some American libraries. Even then progress was painfully slow. The pioneering work of the paper scientists at last bore fruit in an American standard for permanent paper in 1985, and such paper now seems to be widely used.[9] As yet no similar standard has been adopted in the United Kingdom. The Library Association and The Publishers' Association have reached a broad measure of agreement on the subject,[10] but the 'standard' cannot be enforced, although the use of 'acid-free' (i.e. chemically inert) paper is becoming more common.

From a practical point of view, the manifestations and immediate triggers of the decay of paper are perhaps more important than the scientific details of its ultimate causes. Decay caused by a high acid content is most easily identified by the fact that the paper turns brown and becomes brittle. Eventually the paper will disintegrate completely, even without being touched. It has to be emphasized that this process takes place even in environmental conditions which are broadly favourable to paper storage. As we shall see in Chapter Three such conditions rarely exist in major libraries, and the process of decay is therefore exacerbated. The world's libraries and archives are in fact full of documents written and printed on wood-pulp paper which will gradually turn to dust even if they are never used, as the preservation surveys of the last twenty years have so dramatically revealed.

Decay is inherent in the materials of many machine-made papers. There is an additional hazard which is common to all papers, even those which are chemically stable or inert. Because the papermaking process consists of first wetting and then drying the materials, it follows that the wetness or dryness of the paper is critical to its survival. In very dry conditions, paper loses its essential remaining moisture, and becomes brittle. If it is too damp, however, the papermaking process itself is partly reversed, and the paper will begin to disintegrate.

Parchment

Parchment, or vellum (the difference is irrelevant for our purposes), is treated animal skin which can be used for binding or, more frequently, as a writing surface. The skins of sheep, goats and cattle were all used for this purpose. Parchment was first used as a writing material in the middle of the second millennium BC in Egypt, and continued in regular use until the late Middle Ages in western Europe. Indeed, its use for certain legal documents, such as wills, survived the invention of printing. However, it was rarely used for printed books; not only was it far more expensive than paper, even in the fifteenth century, it was also very difficult to print a good impression on its slightly uneven surface. Nevertheless, parchment is, after paper, the substance most commonly found in archives and manuscript collections.

Parchment is prepared by washing the animal skin in water, scraping off the hair and treating the skin with lime; it is not tanned. The skin is then dried at normal temperatures, but under tension on a specially made 'stretching frame'. The result is a material which has a very high tensile strength and is reasonably resilient provided that it is kept dry. Like paper, it will degrade very rapidly if it is damp, because it can absorb large amounts of water quickly, which has the effect of reversing the drying stage of the manufacturing process. Parchment is a stiff substance, far less flexible than leather, but for a writing surface, especially when it is folded and bound, this is, of course, an advantage. In general, parchment documents survive at least as well as those of paper, and indeed good parchment is probably more durable than the cheap printing and writing papers of the last 150 years.[11]

Leather

The pages of a bound book – the 'text-block' – are, of course, protected by the binding. As we shall see, the structural basis of a bookbinding is that the protective outer cover is linked in some way to the text-block. The critical factors in determining the survival properties of a binding are therefore the qualities of the materials which are used and the strength of the linkage between the book and its cover. Like paper, bookbinding materials have chemical characteristics which are crucially significant for preservation.

Until the beginning of the nineteenth century, bookbindings were made completely by hand, using organic materials. The boards were made in the same way, and from the same materials, as paper. The whole construction was covered in treated animal skin, normally calf's leather, although sometimes sheepskin, goatskin or some other material was used. However, from the early nineteenth century onwards, leather began to be displaced by cloths which were made of natural fibres such as cotton and linen.[12]

Leather-covered bookbindings are typical of all collections of books dating from before the early nineteenth century, and indeed for some bindings leather was in use long after the development of bookcloths. The quality of leather, like that of paper, depends largely on the manufacturing process. In leather manufacture, the cleaned skin is tanned, that is to say treated with alkaline chemicals which strengthen it, make it flexible and give it a shiny appearance on the inner (or 'flesh') side. This appearance can be enhanced by subsequent polishing with wax or oils. Good leathers are exceedingly durable, and can survive heavy usage for centuries, but inadequate tanning with poor chemicals will produce leather with little strength.

As in the case of papermaking, the need to meet increased demand led to the use of tanning agents whose product was less durable than their earlier equivalents.[13] This decline began at a much earlier date than in the case of paper. From the mid-seventeenth century onwards, leathers were made which tended to crumble and rot if continuously exposed to certain environmental conditions, especially heat or sunlight. By the middle of the nineteenth century, poor-quality leathers were almost the norm for bookbinding work. Unfortunately, this coincided with a period when many great libraries were organizing the unsorted accumulations of decades or centuries, and the binding programmes which were part of this process made use of very poor, and now badly decayed, leather.

These poor leathers will dry out and turn to a powdery dust if they are consistently too hot, as they are in glass-fronted bookcases exposed to the sun, for example, a situation which was typical of so many country-house libraries in eighteenth- and nineteenth-century England. If storage conditions are damp, the leather may not suffer too badly, but the boards themselves will hydrate and decay, as indeed will the

21

paper. In either case, the result is the same: the binding disintegrates, and is likely to collapse completely when the book is handled. Millions of leather-bound books have lost one board or both, or have split hinges and joints, not because of careless handling but because of the inherent weakness of the materials from which they were made.[14]

Bookcloths

The early nineteenth-century bookcloths, made of high-quality cotton fibre, were in general more satisfactory than much contemporary bookbinding leather. Although cheap cloths do decay, and react particularly badly to damp conditions, they are, for the most part, very stable. The weakness of many nineteenth- and early twentieth-century bindings lies not in the cloth, but in the acidic boards which the cloth covers and in the acidic paper used for the endpapers and spine strips. Modern synthetic polymer 'cloths', while they are not always aesthetically very pleasing, do have a chemical stability denied to many of their organic predecessors.[15]

Adhesives

Synthetic polymers have also largely replaced organic substances in the adhesives used in bookbinding. Traditionally, binders used either water-based paste made from wheat- or rice-flour starches, or glue made from animal derivatives. Pastes are particularly suitable for bookbinding purposes, and indeed many modern conservators will use little else. The animal glues are more problematic; they tend to dry out and become inflexible and will then split when the book is opened. Moreover, some of them are, apparently, regarded as a treat by gourmandizing insects.[16]

Book structures

The structure of the book is as important to its capacity to survive as is the quality of the materials from which it is made. Since about the fourth century AD, virtually all western, and western-influenced, books have been made in the familiar form of the *codex* (Figure 2), in which folded and sewn sheets are protected by an outer covering to which they are attached. Scrolls and rolls, the earlier methods of book construction, survived residually for certain archival purposes, for example the long rolls of parchment which form some medieval English records such as the Pipe Rolls of Exchequer, as well as in the consciously archaic use for copies of the Jewish Talmud for liturgical purposes. For all normal purposes, however, it is the codex structure with which we are

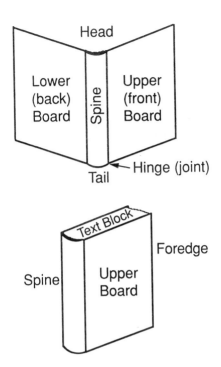

Fig. 2 The codex

concerned.

Until the late nineteenth century, the normal method of bookbinding, now called *craft binding*, created a strong physical link between the text-block and the outer cover. The sheets were folded, put into the correct order ('collated'), in a series of 'gatherings', each of which consisted of a number of folded sheets (from 2 to as many as 32) one inside the other. The gatherings were then sewn. The sewing method changed somewhat over the centuries, but the essence remained the same. A single piece of cotton or linen thread was used for the whole book. It was passed in and out of the centre of each gathering in turn, so that the gathering was held together internally. It was then passed through to the next gathering, so that the gatherings were linked to each other. Between each gathering, in what was to become the spine of the book, it was passed around much thicker cords, or thongs, to give added strength (Figure 3). These thongs were, in due course, passed through

23

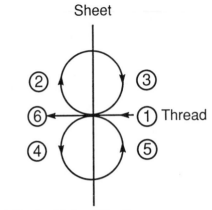

(a) Typical (simplified) sequence
of sewing (side view)

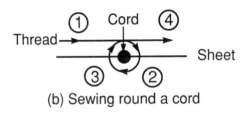

(b) Sewing round a cord

Fig. 3 Sewing

holes in the boards and secured there by knots or wedges, to link the text-block and the cover. Before that was done, however, the text-block itself was beaten with a special hammer along the spine, to give it the rounded shape which is necessary for proper opening of the book; in the same process ('rounding and backing'), recesses were created into which the boards could be placed to form hinges. Endpapers were sewn onto the text-block. Finally, the spine was strengthened and the boards and spine were covered with leather or some other material. The endpapers were pasted down inside the boards, over the knots and wedges at the ends of the sewing thongs. Sometimes the binder left a 'free endpaper' between the pastedown and the first leaf of the book itself.[17] The result was a structure of immense internal strength, which was derived both from sewing and from adhesives.

Craft binding techniques are still used in restoration work, and very occasionally for expensive special editions, but for most purposes other techniques have inevitably displaced them. Almost all hardback books are now 'case bound'. In this process, the text-block and the outer cover, or *case*, are made separately, and brought together only at the last moment. The text-block is sewn, trimmed, and rounded and backed. The endpapers are then attached by means of a thin strip of adhesive, rather than being sewn on. In addition, the spine is strengthened with a piece of strong paper, and with a piece of linen which protrudes a little beyond the edge of the book – the latter is called the 'mull'. The case is machine-made, and consists simply of two boards and a slightly stiffened spine strip, all brought together by being glued to the covering material, normally cloth or some artificial fabric. The endpapers and the mull are then glued to the boards, and the book is complete (Figure 4). Almost the entire process of collation, binding, case-making and casing-in is mechanized, and is almost invariably used for binding the whole print-run of a book, since it is, in effect, a mass-production process.[18]

A third technique, and one widely used for the binding of periodicals or for the rebinding of damaged books, is called 'library binding'. Unlike case-binding, this is not a mass-production process, since individual and differing items are being bound. As a consequence, it offers some of the strengths of traditional craft techniques. In particular, the sewing threads are used to link the text-block and the outer covering, although that covering is really a case rather than the traditional boards.[19]

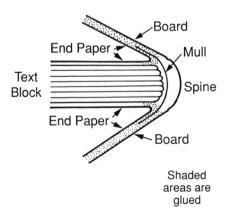

Fig. 4 Casing-in

Unhappily, reference must also be made to 'perfect' binding, a name which describes the precise opposite of this unfortunate technique. The sheets are collated and folded in the usual way, but are then guillotined a millimetre or so in from the fold. The text-block thus becomes a series of single sheets. The outer cover is attached to the 'spine' by adhesives applied under heat and pressure. The resulting 'book' will usually hold together for long enough to be sold, but will rarely survive a single reading. This technique is, happily, largely unknown in Britain, but it is the normal means of binding mass-market paperbacks in the United States. Such books are unsuitable for short-term use, and certainly not for permanent preservation in libraries, although some better techniques are now available. Unfortunately, it is impossible to rebind them conventionally because the gutter through which the sewing thread normally passes has been destroyed. The binder is, therefore, forced to use a technique called 'stab-binding' in which the thread passes through the single sheets at a right angle. It is inelegant, and unsatisfactory for large books, although it has historical precedents, having been used for pamphlets in the seventeenth and eighteenth centuries.[20] It should be added that British and European paperback publishers rarely offend by using perfect bindings. Their products normally have sewn text-blocks which are attached to the outer cover by adhesive at the spine. When good paper and adhesives are used, this creates a surprisingly durable book.

The alternative solution to binding single sheets, often used for archival documents or single printed sheets of historical importance (such as proclamations or broadside ballads) is *guarding*. A guard-book is a library-bound case, with stubs of paper rather than a text-block. The sheets are then glued to the stubs by a thin line of adhesive, and a surprisingly strong book is thus created.[21]

A bookbinding is a mechanical device. It is designed both to protect the text-block, and to give access to it. Access can only be achieved by opening the book, which means that the binding has to be flexible. Ideally, it should allow the book to lie open flat, without any pressure being exerted upon it and without any damage taking place. Some craft bindings achieve this ideal, but they are few, and almost no binding made by any other technique can approach it. A binding is mechanically most vulnerable at the hinges, upon which the boards turn. These are subject to great pressure, so that even in normal and careful use they may eventually break. Careless use, or inferior materials, will hasten their end. In a case-binding, the strength of the hinge ultimately depends on the covering material, since it alone links the boards and the spine. In a craft-bound book, the hinge is, of course, further supported by the cords or thongs, and it is not unusual to see such a book in which the leather has cracked, but the cords are still holding the boards onto the text-block. In case-bound, and to a slightly lesser extent library-bound, books, the strength of the whole structure ultimately depends upon the adhesives, and where inferior adhesives are used, or storage conditions are wrong, the whole structure can collapse.

Non-book materials

Books are, of course, only one part of the contents of almost all libraries. The printed word has been produced in scores of different physical forms. Each presents its own problems to the librarian seeking to preserve it. Periodicals, for example, are issued without permanent bindings, and yet many libraries wish to preserve them in perpetuity. At least that is not inconsistent with the purpose which their publisher had in mind. The same is not true of newspapers, where the librarian is seeking to preserve what is an essentially ephemeral product, with a life-expectancy of less than 24 hours and often produced on correspondingly poor paper. The multifarious forms of print – sheet music, maps, posters and many others – all have their places in the library, and for research libraries which seek to maintain comprehensive collections they present a serious and growing problem. They are produced on the same inherently unstable material as books and journals, and yet in some cases, unlike them, are not even designed for permanent preservation.

Archivists have to cope with even more diverse forms of documents than do librarians. Typing paper, for example, is usually of a fairly poor quality, and yet the 'manuscripts' of many modern literary works exist only in that form. So do millions of letters and other documents worthy of preservation. Even worse is the 'bank' paper used for carbon copies, found in almost all archival collections of modern documents. In the early years of typing, and indeed until after World War II, the quality of the carbon paper was also poor, so that mere legibility, let alone survival, becomes a serious problem. Some carbon images can be erased merely by contact. Photocopies, which have to a large extent displaced carbon copies, are equally problematic. Copies on plain paper, such as are now common, are probably fairly durable, but the early wet-copy processes used paper which decays rapidly and they produced an image which, in many cases, is already faded.

Computer print-out is also to be found in some archival collections. Again, paper quality, especially of the 'listing paper' used in most continuous-feed printers, is poor, and the quality of the image weak. Such print-out is really intended to be temporary, but if it is of archival interest it will have to be preserved in some form. Ironically, in our present state of knowledge even a poor copy on paper is, as we shall see, likely to be more durable than the electronic file which was its source.

Non-printed materials

The printed word is still by far the most important means of information storage and seems likely to continue to be so for the foreseeable future. However, it has never been alone. Print itself never entirely displaced manuscript, and it is itself now being supplemented and partially replaced by photographic and electronic systems. In so far as these 'new' media (several of them actually more than a century old!) contain unique information not stored in printed form, they too will have to be preserved as part of our information resource. Each of them presents its own range of problems, in many cases far more complex than those of print and paper.[22]

Photographic media

Almost all libraries now contain some photographic material. This takes many forms – cine films, slides, microforms, prints and so on. All of these have some common chemical characteristics which determine their capacity to survive. Photographic film and paper are treated with sensitive chemicals upon which a latent image can be implanted when they are exposed to light. Although the details of this process need not concern us, a basic understanding is helpful. Modern photographic materials essentially consist of either two or three layers of substances. The bottom layer is merely a carrier or base, consisting of a cellulose-based film, or paper for a print. The top layer consists of the substance in which the image itself will actually be formed. This substance is metallic, normally silver-based, and it also incorporates the dyes needed for colour reproduction. In films (but not in paper prints) there is a third layer, between these two, which is a binding agent linking the base and the image-forming substance (Figure 5). Additional layers, especially in paper used for prints, consist of chemicals which prevent fading, curling and other faults.

When the top layer is exposed to light, a latent image is formed by

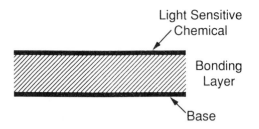

Fig. 5   The structure of film

chemical change. When the film is then 'developed' by being bathed in chemicals, the silver is displaced from the areas which were exposed to light, and the latent image is thus made visible. This visible image is then 'fixed' in a second chemical bath so that it becomes 'permanent', although the extent of the permanence depends upon several factors, including the quality of the chemicals, the water and the film itself, as well as the conditions in which the negative or print is stored. The same essential principles apply to all photographs, whether the material is direct from the camera, or a 'second-generation' copy of the camera film on either film or paper.[23]

There have been many varieties of photographic media. Before cellulose bases, or indeed other 'flexible' films, were commonly used, camera negatives were made on many different bases, including glass and metal. Bases themselves have changed, and older materials still exist in archives. The notorious cellulose nitrate base used for much cine film until the late 1940s, with its dangerous tendency to spontaneous combustion, is still a major problem in film collections. Quite apart from such specific considerations, the chemical base of all photographic materials is susceptible to decay, and images can fade if conditions are not right. Indeed, some images will fade in any conditions, especially those made with the dyes used in early colour films. Some films are more stable than others, and some techniques of processing create a film which has better properties of survival. Broadly speaking, all photographic materials react badly to continuous and excessive light beyond that needed for the use for which they are designed. All need to be carefully handled, since film (as opposed to prints) can be easily and irreversibly damaged. Such damage may even take place in the viewing or projection device which is needed for all photographic images not reproduced on paper, and the creation of the paper image itself requires the use of equipment through which the negative film has to be passed. Film is far less tolerant of heat, light and dust than is paper, and for the librarian who seeks to preserve it as part of a permanent research collection, it presents a major headache.

Recorded sound

Sound recording has a history only slightly shorter than that of photography, although such recordings are perhaps less frequently found in libraries. The most familiar commercial formats – gramophone records, tapes and compact discs – all present preservation problems, but few are intended for permanent retention in libraries. In research collections, where unique material is involved, it is the normal practice to re-record from a master disc or tape, and to make available to users only the copies (or indeed copies of the copies) in order to protect the irreplaceable master. Masters deemed to be of great historical importance are ideally held on tape of the quality used by recording companies and broadcasting organizations for their own archives. Ordinary commercial standard tapes have to be regarded as temporary and disposable, while vinyl records cannot be preserved in perfect condition if they are to be used at all. Compact discs, on the other hand, provided the quality of the data does not deteriorate, seem to be virtually undamageable in a physical sense. In one way or another, therefore, recorded sound does not present serious problems except when it is required for truly archival purposes. In such cases, the storage facilities must take into account the susceptibilities of the various media. Vinyl recordings, for example, react very badly to excessive heat, while any magnetic medium, such as compact disc, is in danger of degradation if it is exposed to a magnetic field.[24]

Electronic media

The third and final group to be considered is that of electronic or digitized media, of which compact disc sound recordings are indeed one example. Others which are in current use are videotape, magnetic tape and magnetic discs (hard and floppy) for storing data inside and outside a computer, pre-recorded compact discs with digitized alpha-numeric data (CD-ROM), videodiscs (which record digitized visual images, without a sound track), compact discs with vision and sound, or with vision sound and digital data (CD-V and CD-I [Interactive] respectively) and various recordable optical discs. No doubt the variety will increase, and the rate of obsolescence of media will continue to be substantial.[25] The permanent preservation of data which are available only in electronic form is a major issue which has still not been fully addressed either professionally or technically.[26] From a purely physical point of view, we know that all electronic storage systems are subject to fairly rapid deterioration, usually within five years. This is to be compared with five hundred years or so for archival microfilm and *de facto* infinity for print. The permanent preservation of electronically encoded data can be guaranteed only by a continuous process of copying and recopying to provide back-up and security discs, a process which seems unlikely to be economically justified for all but a few files of the highest commercial or governmental significance.[27]

One final point remains to be made about the non-printed media. Almost all of them can be accessed only by using specially designed equipment. For most libraries, this will mean little more than a range of easily obtained (if somewhat expensive) current equipment, such as VCRs and CD-players. If original formats are to be preserved, however, it will also be necessary to preserve, *in working order*, the relevant equipment. This problem is particularly acute with recorded sound and the electronic media. For the former, the normal practice is now to digitize as much as possible on compact disc or digitized tape, but this implies an almost continuous process of monitoring and copying.[28] Even so, of course, the original playing equipment must be available for the first transfer to be made. Preserving data available only in machine-readable form is an even greater problem. Computers become obsolescent within five to ten years of manufacture. Transfer to a format compatible with another machine is the only currently available method of permanent preservation of data in an accessible form, and is both expensive and time-consuming.[29]

Conclusion

It was argued that an understanding of the physical nature of information storage materials is fundamental to an understanding of preservation. Although, in the last analysis, it is the information itself which we normally want to preserve, the form in which we store it is critical, because it essentially determines our ability to do so. There will always be some books and documents, and perhaps some other media too, which we wish to preserve in their original physical form for historical reasons. More pertinently, there is at present no technically and economically acceptable medium into which we can transfer even a significant percentage of our store of written and printed information. It seems unlikely that such a medium will exist in the foreseeable future.

Consequently, the preservation of information still depends upon our ability to preserve the books, manuscripts and other documents in which by far the greater part of mankind's collective memory and wisdom is stored. We now know that all of those media are impermanent, but that some are more susceptible to decay than others. We also understand many of the chemical and physical causes of that impermanence. Preservation, therefore, begins with a consideration of how we treat information media in libraries and archives, of how they are stored and used, and, above all, of the environment in which they have to exist.

References

1 On the history of paper, see Hunter, D., *Papermaking. The history and technique of an ancient craft*, 2nd ed., New York, Knopf, 1947, 48 – 63, 224 – 57.

2 Hunter, *Papermaking*, 309 – 40.

3 In the summer of 1988, the present writer saw the traditional methods being used in a village in northern Thailand for making paper for umbrellas.

4 Hunter, *Papermaking*, 170 – 202.

5 Hunter, *Papermaking*, 341 – 73.

6 Priest, D. J., 'Paper and its problems', *Library review*, **36**, 1987, 165.

7 See Brown, L. H., 'Preservation in original format: the role of paper quality' in Smith, *Preservation of library materials*, vol. 1, 52; and Cunha, G. M. and Cunha, D.G., *Libraries and archives conservation: 1980s and beyond*, Metuchen, N J, Scarecrow Press, 1983, 46.

8 Burton, J. O., 'Permanence studies of current commercial book papers', *Bureau of Standards journal of research*, **7**, 1931, 429 – 39.

9 American National Standards Institute, *American National Standard for Information Science – Permanence of paper for printed library materials*, New York, American National Standards Institute (ANSI Z39.48-1984), 1984. But there is still a problem; see Kalina, C. R., 'Acid-free paper for biomedical literature', *Scholarly publishing*, **19**, 1988, 217 – 20.

10 The Library Association, National Preservation Office and The Publishers' Association, *Permanent paper*, London, The Library Association, 1986.

11 Reed, R., *Ancient skins, parchments and leathers*, London, Seminar Press, 1972, 118 – 22.

12 Diehl, E., *Bookbinding. Its background and technique*, 2 vols, New York, Rinehart, 1946, vol. 1, 177 – 80.

13 Clarkson, L. A., 'Developments in tanning methods during the post-medieval period (1500 – 1850)', in East Midlands Industrial Archaeology Conference, *Leather manufacture through the ages*, Leicester, Leicester

University Press, 1983, 11 – 21.

14 For a detailed technical account, see British Leather Manufacturers' Research Association, *The conservation of bookbinding leather*, London, The British Library, 1984.

15 Clough, E. A., *Bookbinding for librarians*, London, Association of Assistant Librarians, 1957, 26 – 34; and Fitzgerald, A., 'Books and bindings', in Swartzburg, S. G. (ed.), *Conservation in the library. A handbook of use and care of traditional and nontraditional materials*, London, Aldwych Press, 1983, 63 – 64.

16 Fitzgerald, 'Books and bindings', 65 – 67.

17 This is a highly simplified account. See Middleton, B. C., *A history of English craft bookbinding technique*, 3rd ed., London, The Holland Press, 1988.

18 Williamson, H., *Methods of book design. The practice of an industrial craft*, 3rd ed., New Haven, Conn., Yale University Press, 1983, 296 – 318.

19 Clough, *Bookbinding for librarians*, 110 – 12.

20 Middleton, *History*, 11 – 12.

21 Clough, *Bookbinding for librarians*, 49.

22 For a general survey, see Harrison, H. P., 'Conservation and audio-visual materials', *Audio-visual librarian*, **13**, 1987, 154 – 62.

23 Hendricks, K. B., *The preservation and restoration of photographic materials in archives and libraries*, Paris, Unesco (PGI-84/WS/1), 1984, 1 – 69, gives a detailed technical account of both contemporary and historical photographic processes.

24 Heckmann, H., 'Storage and handling of audio and magnetic materials', in Smith, *Preservation of library materials*, vol. 2, 67 – 72.

25 Meadows, A.J. 'The medium and the message', in National Preservation Office, *Preservation and technology*, 1 – 9.

26 Sturges, P., 'Policies and criteria for the archiving of electronic publishing', *Journal of librarianship*, **19**, 1987, 152 – 72.

27 For a wide-ranging study, see Hendley, T., *The archival storage potential of microfilm, magnetic media and optical data discs*, Hatfield, National Reprographic Centre for Documentation (BNB Research Fund Report, 10), 1983, 35 – 72.

28 Silver, J. and Stickells, L., 'Preserving sound recordings at the British Library National Sound Archive', *Library conservation news*, **13**, October 1986, 1 – 3.

29 White, S. B. and White, A. E., 'The computer: when tomorrow becomes yesterday', in Swartzburg, *Conservation in the library*, 205 – 19.

3   The environment

The preservation surveys of libraries in industrialized countries in the 1970s revealed the extent of deterioration which had taken place even in comparatively dormant materials. Some of this decay was inevitable, since it was intrinsic to the chemical constitution and physical structure of books. It was also clear, however, that both chemical changes in paper and some of the structural problems of books themselves were being exacerbated by unsatisfactory conditions of storage, and by careless or excessive use. Storage conditions are critical to the survival of books and documents, and although counsels of perfection have to be balanced against the realistically attainable, it is necessary to consider the ideal conditions under which materials ought to be kept, so that we can assess what is acceptable. However, this must be kept in proper perspective. A book kept in the dark, and preferably in a deep-freeze, would never deteriorate, but it would not be of much use. Preservation is, in the last analysis, simply a means of ensuring that information is available when it is needed, and the preservation of the physical object is only one of several means by which that end can be attained. It follows, therefore, that ideal environments, although they might be justified for that tiny minority of books which are art objects or cultural artefacts, have to be reconciled with the conditions in which both librarians and users can work with the books for the purpose for which they were intended, and also with conditions which are technically attainable and economically feasible.

The environmental enemies of books, with which we are concerned in this chapter, are conventionally classified under five broad headings:

- temperature
- humidity
- light
- biological infestation
- pollution

As we shall see, this classification is rather crude, but it is a convenient starting-point, and we shall consider each in turn.

Temperature

The problem of temperature can be stated very simply. All organic materials have a 'preferred' temperature at which their useful life is maximized. A piece of wooden furniture in an overheated room, for example, will eventually dry out and crack and perhaps even disintegrate. Similarly, metal objects will expand, however fractionally, in extremes of temperature. Because these phenomena are understood, there are certain precautions which can be taken to ensure that even though unpreventable change will happen, the usefulness of the object will be preserved. Because it is known that the steel used to make railway lines will expand in high temperatures, engineers leave a small 'expansion joint' between successive rails to allow for this. Despite the precaution, in long periods of hot weather rails will sometimes expand beyond the tolerance allowed and will buckle. Greater tolerances are not acceptable, so that occasional faults have to be expected, and appropriate plans devised to deal with them. The railway engineer, however, has no control over the environment in which the rails are placed; he knows only the probable climatic variations. The librarian or archivist, on the other hand, is dealing with the comparatively closed and controllable environment of a building.

The tolerance of human beings for temperature variations is fairly limited. The full range of temperatures known to scientists is from absolute zero (– 273.15°C) to the alleged temperature at the centre of the sun (in excess of 15 million°C). In practice people can survive only in a minute part of this range, from about – 10°C to about 50°C. Human tolerance is slightly increased by the use of special clothing and equipment, but, in effect, beyond these limits a person can survive (in space or under the sea, for example) only by carrying a micro-environment in the form of a completely enclosed suit of some kind and adequate supplies of air. Most people feel 'comfortable' in an even smaller range of temperatures, from about 12°C to about 21°C, although this varies according to habit and familiarity. A person from a tropical country may 'feel cold' at a temperature as high as 20°C, a level which a native of north-west Europe would regard as agreeably warm. Since libraries are for people, the ambient temperature has to be within the small range which their staff and users prefer; there are inevitable slight variations which reflect local expectations of 'normal' conditions.

Modern technology has given us far greater control over the internal environment of buildings. We can regulate the air temperature to within one or two degrees, and it can be monitored so that it remains roughly constant even if extreme changes take place outside the building. This capacity is a fairly new phenomenon. As recently as twenty years ago, it was not unusual for the interior spaces of buildings to be colder in winter than they were in summer; their occupants took the simple expedient of wearing more or fewer clothes, or garments made of heavier or lighter fabrics, according to the season. In western Europe and North America this practice has now almost entirely vanished, even domestically, and heavy clothes are reserved for outdoor use. We have increased the average internal temperature of our buildings by as much as 5°C or even 10°C, and our social habits have changed accordingly. We eat less, and we wear fewer and lighter clothes. We move from heated houses, in heated cars, to heated offices; we do our shopping in enclosed and heated malls and heated shops. We expect all public buildings and enclosed spaces to be heated for our convenience and we act accordingly. Libraries are no exception.

If central heating has increased the temperature in buildings in temperate countries, air-conditioning has had the opposite effect in hot climates. Of course, hundreds of millions of people lived in the very hot parts of the globe long before any artificial cooling systems were available, and indeed they still do so where such systems are not in use. Nevertheless, long before Europeans had penetrated to those parts of the world, the inhabitants who had the power and the money designed buildings which were intended to be cool such as the traditional Arabian houses with open central courtyards and very high windowless walls. Builders used psychological tricks to give the impression of coolness, such as the fountains and gardens in Moghul or ancient Persian architecture. Occupants employed servants to circulate the air using fans. Europeans followed all of these practices when they settled in the tropics, but the truth is that it is only since the invention of air-conditioning that such climates have become truly tolerable to most people accustomed to temperate climates. The massive development of the 'Sun Belt' states of the south-western USA since 1945 reflects the success of air-conditioning systems in making these hot and inhospitable desert places habitable by people who can afford to create the climate in which they want to live.

The demand for increases in the temperatures in buildings has affected libraries, as it has other places. Indeed, public demand is to some extent reflected in the law, which in some countries, including the United Kingdom, regulates the minimum permitted temperatures for spaces in which employees are required to work. Modern library buildings have central heating systems or air-conditioning systems incorporated in the design, and many older buildings have had such systems installed. The results are generally very pleasant for staff and users. For the books they have been catastrophic.

The basic scientific reason for this catastrophe can be stated very simply. The speed of chemical reactions increases with rises in temperature. In general, it approximately doubles with every rise of 10°C. The rate of increase in the deterioration of paper is even faster, doubling for every increase of approximately 4°C.[1] Deterioration is manifest in two ways. First, the acid in the paper reacts with such catalysts as atmospheric pollutants or the water content in the air; this breaks down the cellulose which bonds together the fibres in the paper. Secondly, a process of oxidation can take place in certain circumstances, especially with prolonged exposure to light, in which residual metals in the paper will degrade both the lignin and the cellulose, and hence weaken the chemical structure of the paper, perhaps fatally.[2] These processes of degradation can be inhibited or delayed by controlling other environmental conditions, but high temperatures will always exacerbate the effects of all the inherent chemical problems of paper, even in high-quality 'acid-free' or chemically inert paper.

There is no 'ideal' temperature for paper, and for the cheap acidic paper which was used for so many nineteenth- and early twentieth-century books and documents no regulation of temperature can prevent inevitable eventual destruction. However, it is possible to delay the inevitable by careful temperature controls, and to do so within limits which are broadly acceptable to both staff and users. One crucial point is that *changes* in temperature are, if anything, more damaging than a consistently high temperature. Thus to move a book from a coolish air-conditioned store to a heated reading room can do more damage than to have the storage area slightly overheated. In broad terms, paper will tolerate a temperature of about 20 – 22°C, provided that the air is fairly dry. This is acceptable to people, and attainable in most buildings in which the ambient temperature can be regulated. Ideally, the temperature should be somewhat lower, perhaps as low as 15°C or even a little less. The relevant British Standard suggests that the temperature for the storage of paper and parchment in archives should be in the range 13 – 18°C.[3] In practice, this can be attained only for rarely used materials in storage areas in which there is only an occasional human presence, since such a temperature would now be regarded as being too 'cold' for a working environment.

In practice, paper is quite tolerant within these broad limits. For non-paper media, storage temperatures are far more critical. For example, modern PVC gramophone records can, in theory, tolerate up to about 50°C, but in practice begin to warp at a considerably lower temperature if they are consistently stored in such heat. In practice, about 20°C, with as little variation as possible, is recommended.[4] Electronic and magnetic media are even more sensitive. The magnetic media, both audio tape and the magnetic discs and tapes used for the storage of digitized data outside a computer, also need to be kept at constant and controlled temperatures. In fact, humidity control is probably even more important than simple temperature control in these cases. Indeed, problems of long-term preservation of these media are still unsolved, and at present they can really be regarded only as temporary storage systems. Data which exist only on magnetic media need to be regularly copied in order to ensure their long-term survival without degradation.[5] Optical discs, and the technologically similar compact audio discs, seem to have greater potential as long-term preservation media, being more tolerant of their ambient environment, although the testing procedures which have been used to establish their lifetimes seem to be open to some question.

Photographic film is the most sensitive medium of all. The maximum temperature at which celluloid film can be stored for archival purposes is 21°C, and it has very little tolerance of temperature change. More than ± 4°C will cause near-fatal problems, so that a constant temperature is more than merely an ideal if the objective is long-term preservation. Processed colour film is most sensitive of all, but prints can tolerate slightly higher temperatures of up to about 25°C.[6] For long-term storage (for archival master negatives, for example), very low-temperature conditions, of below 2°C, are normally recommended.[7]

Humidity

Temperature is only one aspect of the ambient environment in a building. The other is humidity, the quantity of water in the air. This is measured as *relative humidity*. Relative humidity (RH) is defined as the percentage of the quantity of water in a particular volume of air in relation to the maximum quantity which it can hold at its present temperature. Thus an RH level of 100% represents complete saturation (outdoors in heavy rain, for example), while 0% is completely dry (approached only in desert conditions). The natural range of RH in buildings in temperate countries is probably between about 30% and 60%. However, the RH can be modified by mechanical devices. Dehumidifiers remove excess moisture from the air, and can be used on a very small scale (as in a damp room), or on a large scale throughout a building as part of an air-conditioning system. To solve the opposite problem, humidifiers can increase the moisture levels in very dry air. Air-conditioning systems normally incorporate humidity controls, so that in practice humidity and temperature are regulated together.

To human beings, the perceptions of humidity and temperature are closely associated; there is indeed a scientific link between them. High temperatures and high levels of RH are perhaps the least comfortable circumstances in which we normally find ourselves. Such conditions are common in some equatorial countries, such as Singapore, Thailand, parts of central Africa and large areas of Latin America, and they occur intermittently even in temperate climates such as north-west Europe during the summer. More dramatically, in continental climatic conditions, such as those in the Midwest of the United States, hot and humid conditions in summer alternate with very cold winters. Mark Twain described the climate of Chicago, which has precisely these conditions, as 'nine months of winter and three months of hell'. We also find combinations of high RH and low temperatures; this is the condition loosely called 'damp' by most people. More rarely, we encounter the high temperatures and low RH associated with the Middle East or the American south-west. In order to create a fully controlled environment, an air-conditioning system has to be able to regulate both temperature and humidity to pre-determined levels.

The 'wrong' RH can lead to serious and irreversible damage to paper and other information storage materials. Briefly, if conditions are too dry, paper will become embrittled, while if they are too damp, fungal moulds will develop. The opposite extreme of very dry conditions generally exists only in hot desert areas. Fortunately, libraries have been established in such regions only recently, and, like other buildings, are typically equipped with excellent air-conditioning systems. Provided the system is functioning properly, there is no serious problem of dryness inside the building.

It is the excessively damp conditions which are both more common and more problematical. The basic physical facts can be stated simply. The moisture in the air will be partially transferred to all absorbent

39

('hygroscopic') substances with which it is in contact. Paper is hygroscopic, and excessive damp will, in effect, reverse the papermaking process by putting back into the paper some of the water which was removed from it as the pulp was being dried. When paper does become too damp, it attracts the microbiological organisms which manifest themselves as mould. This can migrate from the paper itself through the boards and even into wooden shelves. Moreover, it is a particular problem of handmade paper, in whose manufacture the drying process was generally less effective than the artificial heat used in Fourdrinier machines.

Damp is a major problem for libraries and archives in many parts of the world, and especially for the great historic research libraries and archival repositories of Europe. Their massive collections on handmade paper are in serious danger from mould damage if climatic conditions are not properly controlled. In temperate climates, and especially in north-west Europe, dampness is often found in the older buildings in which many major libraries and repositories are still housed. Buildings are inevitably subject to damp after centuries of existence and because some of them are, quite rightly, historic monuments as well as working libraries there may even be legal limits within which any structural alterations or visible modifications have to take place. Many smaller collections, such as those of cathedrals or country houses, are housed in similar buildings, with the added complication that in some cases their owners are unable to bear the considerable costs of whatever environmental improvements might be achieved. Mould can and does develop in cold and damp conditions, and dehumidification is essential if serious trouble is to be avoided. Once microbiological damage takes place it can rarely be reversed.

The humidity problem in tropical and subtropical regions is even more dramatic, if only because it is universal. Heat and humidity promote the development of moulds at an uncontrollable rate, and libraries and archives in such places face a major difficulty. This is exacerbated when, as is the case in many developing countries, funds cannot be made available from limited national resources for the installation and very heavy running costs of elaborate air-conditioning systems. In any case, many collections have spent decades or even centuries in unsuitable conditions before they ever reach the comparative safety of a public repository. Control can only be achieved by eliminating the worst affected materials, which may at least prevent the further spread of mould, and then by creating a micro-climate in which materials of exceptional importance can be housed.

Mould growth takes place at any temperature in a range from 15 to 35°C, although it seems to be at its worst at about 30°C. There is a similarly wide range of RH levels at which mould growth will occur in higher temperatures, from about 45% to about 60%, although laboratory experiments suggest that, fortunately, development is at its worst only when an exceptionally high 75% of RH is reached. There is a direct and significant relationship between temperature change and the moisture levels in hygroscopic materials. As warm air is cooled, it deposits some of its moisture content, which is absorbed by any hygroscopic materials with which it comes into contact. Thus, cooling the air by 4°C can raise the RH by as much as 10%. In other words, if the temperature is to be controlled by reducing it to acceptable levels for books and users alike, the RH must also be controlled to ensure that the books do not absorb the surplus moisture which the air extrudes as the temperature falls. Again, this is a particular problem in tropical countries, where RH is naturally about 60% for much of the time, and the temperature an uncomfortable 30°C or more.[8]

It is even more difficult to define an 'ideal' RH than it is to define an 'ideal' temperature. Indeed the two cannot in practice be wholly disentangled. Where a full environmental control system is available, the recommended level of RH for a library is between 55% and 65%, provided that the temperature is held between 13 and 18°C.[9] It is doubtful whether this counsel of perfection can be attained in most libraries, but ensuring a constant RH, at a reasonable level, is probably more important than absolute precision in attaining an ideal percentage.

Maintaining an acceptable level of RH is important for paper and parchment, but, as with temperature levels, for photographic materials it is critical. Moulds can develop on photographic film, while the paper on which prints are made is, of course, subject to the same problems as other paper. For film, however, a much more important problem is that a constantly high level of RH will break down the gelatin size which is used as a divider between the layers of chemical of which film consists. The effect is that the film 'melts'; the image consequently disintegrates long before any mould spores have an opportunity to develop. An RH of 60% is the absolute maximum permissible for film storage and use, even if only short-term preservation is envisaged. For long-term preservation of archival master negatives of research materials, it is almost impossible for the RH to be too low. In practice, a range of 15% to 40% is acceptable for monochrome microfilm, and up to

50% for other monochrome films. For colour films and diazo films, however, the upper limit is substantially lower, being no more than 30%. In fact, for long-term security, storage at near-zero temperature and RH is probably the best method, the ideal combination being perhaps 2°C and 2% RH.[10] This, of course, can only be attained for the archival masters, since the internegatives (i.e. negative copies of the master for ordinary use) and positives which are used for copying and reading or projection have to be maintained at a temperature and RH comparable with that of the studio, reading area or projection room, since sudden change will cause even greater damage.

Light

Humidity and temperature are the two major natural obstacles to the permanent preservation of paper and parchment. An excessive level of light can also cause damage, but it is especially serious, as might be expected, in the case of photographic materials. The damage inflicted on paper by excessive light is chemical. Ultraviolet radiation, found both in sunlight and in artificial fluorescent light, contributes to the breakdown of the cellulose structures in the paper. It is also the direct cause of the fading of pigments (such as those used in the illumination and rubrication of manuscripts), of inks and of dyes in colour film and photographic prints. In addition, of course, direct sunlight raises the air temperature, especially if it passes through glass, and all conventional artificial lighting systems generate some heat which radiates from the light source.

The ideal level of lighting for the storage of library materials of all kinds is total darkness, but it is only in closed stack areas this can be attained. It is a sensible economy measure, quite apart from being desirable, to ensure that closed-access stacks are lit only when they are in use by book fetchers, except for the any legally required minimum level of emergency or security lighting. Stack lighting, consisting of fluorescent tubes fitted with ultraviolet filters and diffusers, presents no real preservation problems if it is sensibly and economically used. Reading areas are more difficult. Readers need appropriate levels of light for working. For areas in which old or fragile materials are used, fluorescent lighting (which generates comparatively little heat), with ultraviolet filters, is probably the most suitable system, and is certainly the cheapest to operate. If there are windows in reading areas or stacks, it is essential that they too have ultraviolet filters in or on the glass. As in so many other aspects of preservation, we have to be realistic and sensible about this. Libraries cannot expect users or staff to work in Stygian gloom. The ultimate objective of preservation is to facilitate, not to inhibit, the use of materials, but to do so in circumstances which are consistent with the continued existence of the materials themselves. Moderate but acceptable levels of filtered light will achieve precisely this.[11]

With photographic materials, we have a different problem. Monochrome film which has been processed to archival standards suffers little from light. Colour film, transparencies and prints, however, are very sensitive. Theoretically, this could be a serious obstacle to preservation, and certainly should be considered in, for example, planning to use first-generation colour photographs in a long-term exhibition. In practice, however, photographic materials in libraries and archives are normally stored in total darkness, usually in boxes, albums or folders, which are themselves kept in filing cabinets. Short-term exposure for viewing or projection causes no appreciable damage.[12]

Biological infestation

Because the most common material in a library – paper – is organic, it is subject to biological infestation by mould spores and by insects which are attracted to the its chemical constituents as a medium for growth or as food. Mould has already been mentioned in considering the problems arising from excessive humidity. Insect infestation needs to be considered separately. While this is a problem which is at its worst in libraries and archives in tropical countries, it is certainly not unique to them. Indeed, various silverfish, cockroaches and so-called 'bookworms' are comparatively common, especially in older buildings in temperate countries. The various species of insects have slightly different tastes; some prefer paper, while some choose to dine off binding adhesives or even sewing threads. Some particularly fastidious gourmets select a particular kind of paper, such as 'art' paper with a high china clay content in its glazed surface.[13]

The elimination of insect infestation is an expensive undertaking for which outside specialists would normally have to be employed. As always in library preservation, prevention is better than having to find – and to fund – a cure. A number of comparatively simple measures can dramatically reduce the likelihood of insect problems. The elimination of vegetable matter from the library and its outer walls is one factor. Planters and flower displays inside, and creepers growing on the outside walls, may be aesthetically pleasing, but they encourage insects. If they cannot be eliminated they have to be monitored. The proper care of all the wooden parts of the library, whether structural or in the form of furniture or shelving, is also critical, since termites breed in wood. It is particularly important in tropical countries to ensure that, as far as possible, the library building is inaccessible not only to termites, but also to cockroaches and to the rodents which inevitably abound in such climates. The well-sealed buildings with which we are familiar in temperate regions are neither normal nor indeed climatically necessary in hotter countries, especially where air-conditioning is not an economic possibility. The only option open to the librarian or archivist in such circumstances is to ensure that the books and documents are regularly monitored, and that prompt measures are taken to deal with infestation.

Pollution

The final and most dramatic hazard, and one which exacerbates all the others, is that of pollution. The pollution of the environment has, of course, become a major political issue in many countries during the last decade, and some small steps are being taken to alleviate it. Nevertheless, it is, and will continue to be, a serious danger to both life and property, especially in heavily populated urban areas. Atmospheric pollution has been a consequence of industrialization ever since man first made fire and filled his cave with smoke. It is unavoidable in the modern world, and all we can do is try to contain it at acceptable levels and deal with the consequences of what remains.

Historically, the major pollutant in industrialized countries was in the form of the sulphur products of coal burning. For more than a century, coal was the principal fuel for transport, machinery, heating and the generation of other forms of power such as gas and electricity. The grime which accumulated on buildings in cities such as London and Paris took decades to remove when coal burning was forbidden or became economically less attractive. The similar patina of grime on books and documents has proved more persistent even if it is less visible, although a century ago it had already been noted as a significant 'enemy' of books.[14] Today, coal burning has been largely eliminated from urban areas in the west, although it continues elsewhere in the world, as well as in major facilities such as coal-fired power-stations. Smoke has been replaced as the major hazard by the carbon monoxide which is the major constituent of the exhaust gases of petrol-driven internal combustion engines, and by the by-products of petrol combustion, especially compounds of lead.

The effects of various pollutants on library and archival materials can be very severe indeed. At the simplest level, dirt is not only unsightly but damaging. Particles of dust can cause physical damage to paper. If the RH is high, the dust may become even more hygroscopic than the paper and consequently accelerate the degradation of the cellulose structure. Terms like 'dust' and 'dirt' are, of course, very imprecise. These particles are themselves chemicals which may, for example, contain fragments of lead from combusted petrol or alkaline dust from cement on a building site. Each particular kind of 'dust' sets up its own chemical reactions, although the general effects are the same, and they are all almost equally deleterious. Oxidation by sulphur dioxide or carbon monoxide can break down cellulose and hence exacerbate the deterioration of paper and parchment. Not all such chemical pollutants are external to the materials themselves. Some synthetic polymers, used in films, magnetic tape and indeed in paper, may contain minute quantities of chemical impurities which can lead to internal breakdown of the molecular structure. This is fortunately avoidable and rare, for the use of high-quality film and tape (the media in which the main problems are concentrated) effectively eliminates this particular hazard.

The control of the air quality in a library building is important for people as well as materials. Again, a fully functional air-conditioning system is the ideal solution, since it will filter and purify the air as well as control the temperature and humidity. Where this is not practicable for the whole building, it may be possible to create smaller controlled environments, such as a room or even a cupboard, for materials of exceptional importance or great vulnerability.[15] Security copies of computer tapes, for example, are normally stored in a completely controlled environment. A library may well feel that the master copy of its catalogue deserves this treatment in view of the cost of replacement in case of loss or damage. More traditionally, a book or manuscript of exceptional value might be exhibited to the public only in an environmentally controlled display case. Control of the external environment is ultimately beyond the power of the librarian or archivist, but it is necessary to be aware of it, especially if there are any hazards and sudden changes such as construction work.

Conclusion
In broad terms, it is not difficult to define the ideal conditions for the storage of library and archival materials. However, those ideal conditions can conflict both with what is attainable and indeed with what is

acceptable to those people who use and work with the collections. Neither staff nor users can work properly in cold and dark conditions, and should not be expected to do so. We have to reconcile the ideal with the practicable, and try to achieve an ambient environment in which materials will not suffer more than unavoidable damage. If a building is kept at about 20°C, with an RH of about 45%, little harm will come to most materials while most people will be reasonably comfortable. If the air can also be kept clean, so that neither atmospheric pollution nor infestation by insects or rodents is likely to happen, then the collection will be physically as stable and well protected as a working collection can be.

Of course, for some special materials, added protection is desirable. Cultural heritage objects, or historical research materials of great importance, whose physical preservation is deemed to be essential, will have to be protected more stringently. Indeed, they may be made available to users only in surrogate form or under very carefully controlled conditions. In some cases, the information medium itself may dictate the conditions in which it is kept. Colour film and magnetic tape, for example, both require special conditions if their useful life is to be maximized, and the tolerances for these media are far more critical than those for paper or parchment. However, the basic principles of physical conservation are clear enough. A building which is clean, dry and not overheated will not destroy its contents.

The design, use and maintenance of the building is an integral part of a preservation programme, for those factors effectively define the immediate environment in which the materials are stored and, in the case of non-circulating collections, used. In the inevitably rare circumstance of a new building being planned, the librarian or archivist will wish to ensure that the basic design is conceived with the preservation of materials in mind. Where funding is available, full environmental controls throughout the building are the ideal, although it has to be remembered that the functioning of the building, the maintenance of its contents and the comfort of its staff and users then become wholly dependent upon the efficient operation of that system. A poor installation, or one which frequently breaks down, is worse than none at all. In countries with unreliable power supplies, for example, or where spare parts or skilled labour for repair work may be in short supply, adaptations of traditional local building designs can sometimes be far better than a western-style building. High ceilings, with or without fans, shaded windows which do not allow direct sunlight to fall on books or readers, and similar traditional practices, are far more effective protectors of the collection than hermetically sealed buildings in which the temperature and humidity will rise almost uncontrollably if the environmental control systems fail.

In the existing buildings in which most libraries are housed, the environment can be controlled to some extent even without a full air-conditioning system or anything approaching one. Air pollution, heat and light can all be regulated by simple and comparatively inexpensive means. There is no reason why any library should be dirty; the regular cleaning of books and shelves is a basic procedure in any preservation programme. Windows can be shaded, and, where necessary, screened against flying insects when they are open. Both the level and the sources of artificial light can be regulated. Fitting ultraviolet filters to existing lights is cheap and easy; ensuring that the level of light is no more than is necessary for comfortable working conditions is economically desirable, quite apart from any other consideration. Heating systems, if properly maintained, can normally be regulated to within about $\pm$ 3°C, which should be adequate for most normal preservation purposes. Excessive humidity, especially that of cold damp in older buildings, is more of a problem, but dehumidifiers can help on a small scale, even if they cannot cope with a very large damp space. Proper building maintenance really requires the elimination of large damp areas by other means, for the sake of the building itself as well as its contents. In short, the control of the environment is not beyond the capacity of most libraries or record repositories.

We can define the precise scientific parameters within which materials ought to be stored and housed, but in practice these parameters are almost meaningless. Libraries are for use, and even great research collections want to attract readers. Unless materials are to be made wholly inaccessible – which can be justified only in a very few cases – we have to accept a working compomise between the ideal and the permissible. If that is achieved, little harm will be done and much quiet good will be the result.

References

1 Smith, M. A., 'Care and handling of bound materials', in Smith, *Preservation of library materials*, vol. 2, 51.
2 Priest, 'Paper and its problems', 169 – 73.
3 British Standards Institution, *Recommendations for the storage and exhibition of archival documents*, London, British Standards Institution (BS 5454:1977),

1977, para. 9.2.

4   Heckmann, 'Storage and handling of audio and magnetic materials', in Smith, *Preservation of library materials*, vol. 2, 67 – 71; and Hendley, *Archival storage potential*, 35 – 45.

5   Meadows, 'Medium and the message', in National Preservation Office, *Preservation and technology*, 6.

6   Hendricks, K. B., 'Storage and handling of photographic materials', in Smith, *Preservation of library materials*, vol. 2, 58, 61, 62; and Hendricks, *The Preservation and restoration*, para. 11.2.3.

7   Hendricks, *Preservation and restoration*, para. 11.2.4.

8   Wood Lee, M., *Prevention and treatment of mold in library collections with an emphasis on tropical climates. A RAMP study*, Paris, Unesco (PGI-88/WS/9), 1988, 12 – 3, 21 – 2.

9   BS 5454:1977, para. 9.2.

10   Hendricks, *Preservation and restoration*, 72 – 4.

11   Smith, 'Care and handling', in Smith, *Preservation of library materials*, 51 – 3.

12   Hendricks, *Preservation and restoration*, para. 11.2.7

13   For a detailed survey, see Parker, T. A., *Study on integrated pest management for libraries and archives. A RAMP study*, Paris, Unesco (PGI-88/WS/20), 1988, 9 – 49.

14   By William Blades in his pioneering *The enemies of books*, London, Elliot Stock, 1888, cited by Swartzburg, S. G., 'General care', in Swartzburg, *Conservation in the library*, 8, 27 (n.3).

15   Pascoe, M. W., *Impact of environmental pollution on the preservation of archives and records: a RAMP study*, Paris, Unesco (PGI-88/WS/18), 1988, 13 – 23.

4 *Preservation policy and library use*

The preservation problem in libraries and archives has a physical origin. The paper, parchment and other materials upon which information is stored are subject to deterioration at a rate which is influenced by the environment in which they are kept and used. Preservation cannot be expected simply to happen; it has to be directed like any aspect of library activity. A preservation policy is needed which will determine priorities and methods, if only to ensure that limited funds are not dissipated on work of little or no value. Policies have to be based on an understanding of principles, but also derive from a knowledge of local circumstances and from a broader concept of the function of the institution. All of these factors have to be taken into account in evolving a preservation policy. As we have seen, comparatively few British libraries have yet recognized the need for formal policy statements, although probably more now have a preservation policy than the raw data might suggest.

The basic objective of a preservation policy can be defined as being to ensure that materials and information which the library's users can reasonably demand will be available when they are needed. Hence it must be based on an understanding of three related factors:

- the demands of the library's clients
- the intellectual quality of the existing stock
- the use of information and the literature which contains it.

A fourth factor is the physical condition of the collection and the buildings in which it is housed. While this is not subordinate to the first three, it nevertheless depends upon them, for until the use and quality of the stock is understood, there can be no effective guidelines for interpreting the results of a physical survey, or even for determining which parts of the collection shall be the subject of such a survey.

The demands of clients
All libraries have a more or less clear idea of the client group at which

their services are principally aimed. The public library is the most comprehensive, with its avowed intention of serving all the inhabitants of a particular area, and of providing them with everything from leisure reading to high-level information services. Within a large public library system there are obviously significant variations in the use of particular services and the functions of particular branches, but the aim of a comprehensive service is constant. Other types of library have more limited client groups whose information and literature needs can be more specifically defined and perhaps therefore more easily met. The library of a school, college or university, for example, primarily exists to serve the members of the institution, both teachers and students. Its services are defined by the needs of these clients, and its holdings largely determined by their interests. This is even more true in a special library, whether private or public, which exists for the sole purpose of serving a very well-defined, and perhaps very small, client group, whose needs are very specific. External services may be offered, but they are secondary and often part of mutually beneficial co-operative schemes.

Of course, there is overlap of both use and purpose. Those with access to a university library may well make use of public libraries for their leisure reading; the employees of organizations with special libraries may have access to a university library for books and information not available to them directly, and so on. Similarly, some university libraries (although only a very few) see themselves solely as providers of textbooks and current information rather than, to a greater or lesser extent, long-term archival institutions in which at least a part of the holdings is intended for permanent preservation. On the other hand, there are some collections in public libraries which are clearly of permanent interest and importance, and for which long-term preservation is essential. No general rules can be suggested. It is for each library, in consultation with its clients and its funding body, to define its own objectives. It is within the parameters suggested by these objectives that a preservation policy has to be evolved and implemented.

The quality of the stock

The objective measurement of the intellectual quality of the stock is an essential element in determining a preservation policy. The random preservation of individual items which have no context in the collection is a waste of limited resources. Stock assessment has, until recently, been a somewhat subjective exercise, at the level of 'we have always been strong in X'. Such statements from long-established members of staff with a deep knowledge of the collections are not to be despised, but they can hardly form the basis of an objective evaluation of the library's holdings. The system known as 'Conspectus', developed by the members of the Research Libraries Group (RLG) in the United States, is one attempt to overcome the problem of excessive subjectivity.

The basic principle of Conspectus is both simple and attractive. The existing collection is assessed using such criteria as language coverage (English only; all western languages, etc.), format (books and journals; books only; all formats, etc.) and intellectual level or scope (textbooks; research monographs, etc.). These are recorded by means of codes on a form which also allows for the use of 'Scope notes' to add more sophisticated comments. The Conspectus is divided into subject areas using a standard classification scheme. Thus a library can arrive at an evaluation of its collection which will, for example, indicate that in DDC class 020 it has a collection at Level 4 ('Research Level'). This, therefore, contains all the major works in the field, including specialized monographs, a comprehensive collection of indexes, bibliographies and abstracts and a wide range of primary and secondary journals. The subject areas are defined, as in this example, by the broad use of a classification system. In the RLG version this was, inevitably, Library of Congress, although Dewey has been used in the United Kingdom and elsewhere.[1]

For the most part, Conspectus has been applied in academic and research libraries. Indeed, the original concept within RLG was that Conspectus would provide a means of comparing collections and co-ordinating collection development policies between certain libraries within the Group. The format was devised so that the Conspectus could be mounted on the RLIN (Research Libraries Information Network) data base, and it was as a tool of collaboration that Conspectus was presented to the profession at large.[2] However, there is no reason in principle why it should not be used in any kind of library, and for purely internal purposes. In the United Kingdom, the British Library has undertaken a substantial exercise as part of a larger review of its collection development policy.[3] By far the most active British project, however, has been that at the National Library of Scotland, where Conspectus has been used internally, and also to give a broader picture of the holdings of Scottish academic libraries and research collections.[4] Elsewhere in the world Conspectus has been applied in libraries which are trying to reassess both their strengths and their priorities. The State Library of New South Wales in Australia has made notable advances on this front, although it has, as have both the British Library and the Scottish team, adapted the RLG scheme to local circumstances and needs.[5]

The relevance of Conspectus to preservation lies in its apparently unprecedented power as a tool for collection management. The existing collection can be measured against a library's collecting objectives, which can themselves be defined in the same terms of language, scope and level. A direct, if somewhat crude, comparison is then possible between objectives and achievements. Where the two do not correspond, collection development policies and acquisitions can be adjusted accordingly. In the financial circumstances which prevail in most libraries today, this is likely to mean in practice that there is a more effective mechanism for the management of contraction; even that, however, is better than unregulated and inconsistent individual decisions on withdrawal without replacement, cancellation of subscriptions and so on. Similarly, when the quality of the collection has been assessed, and the future pattern of development of particular parts of it determined, better decisions can be taken about the preservation of existing stock and future acquisitions. If it is determined that a particular subject area is already at Research Level, and is to be maintained and developed at that level, then it follows that the bulk, and perhaps all, of the holdings in that field are intended for permanent retention. The exceptions (duplicate copies of textbooks, for example) will be few and minor. If these materials, and older materials already in the library, are to be retained for research purposes, then it follows that more preservation efforts will have to be directed towards them than towards other areas of the collection which have been determined to have a lesser value in that particular library. This approach has been criticized as a 'blunt instrument',[6] and it is certainly not perfect; it has particularly serious limitations in dealing with very specialized collections, or with subjects in which journal literature is more significant than monographs. Even so, there is growing evidence that, when it is used with discretion, Conspectus can be a useful instrument in a collection management programme and can have valuable implications for preservation policy.

The use of information
Preservation is not an antiquarian exercise for keeping objects from the past simply because they are old. It is a managerial tool for making information available to users. The basic issues of preservation policy can therefore best be stated in terms of the intended or predicted use

of the materials. We can reduce these issues to three fundamental questions:

- What is to be preserved?
- For how long is it to be preserved?
- By what means is it to be preserved?

The answers to these three questions provide the foundations upon which a preservation policy can be built, but each answer requires an understanding of a wide range of issues about the library as a whole.

What is to be preserved: the issue of selection
It is both impossible and undesirable to preserve everything in its original physical form. Even if it were possible, it would be impracticable for all libraries to do so because of limitations of space. If the collection is to be properly developed and managed, there must be a process of selection for preservation. From this there follows the somewhat less palatable conclusion that some items are effectively being selected for non-preservation, although this can be at several different levels, as we shall see.

How is this selection to take place, and what factors are to be considered? Four basic parameters can be suggested:

- subject
- format
- age
- use

The subject of a book is fundamental to the decision to acquire it for a library, and equally so to the decision to retain or dispose of it.[7] Within an individual library, the decision can be taken that a particular field is of such importance to clients that all materials in that field have to be preserved. In due course, this may come to be treated as a 'special collection', and, indeed, in the long term, all material intended for permanent preservation will have to be subjected to 'special' treatment of some kind.

The format or medium may in itself define the practicability of preservation. As we have seen, some of the magnetic media cannot be preserved with any guarantee of data integrity for more than a few years, just as items printed on acidic and embrittled paper will eventually disintegrate. Preservation policy must therefore define what categories of information are to be preserved even though that information exists

53

only in a comparatively unstable medium. The implication is that the information will be transferred to another medium (from paper to film, for example) or be copied regularly (from disc to disc, for example) to ensure its survival.

The age of the material can be a determining factor in several ways. A research library may decide, as a matter of principle, to preserve all books printed before a certain date, even if surrogates are made or acquired to protect the originals from over-use. This is increasingly the case with historic newspaper collections in British libraries. At the other extreme, it may be felt that some categories of material can be disposed of when they reach a pre-determined age, because their use, in that particular library, can be regarded as ended. For example, public libraries do not generally keep runs of all the national newspapers to which they subscribe, often in multiple copies, for daily use.

Most important of all, however, and most neglected in this context, is the factor of use. Materials which are wanted and used by the library's clients have to be preserved, or acceptable substitutes provided. Other materials may be permitted to survive, but utility has to be the ultimate determinant of preservation.[8] Of course, further definition is needed. Acceptable levels of use can legitimately vary from many times a day to a few times in a century. Crude measures cannot be applied, but where it can be shown that materials are unlikely ever again to be used in a particular library, and there is no other reason (such as age) for preserving them, then it is legitimate to regard them as candidates for disposal or 'benign neglect'. On the other hand, even a low level of scholarly use of material may justify preservation in some form if the collection is important or unique,[9] and it has recently been argued that the concept of 'benign neglect' needs to be reconsidered.[10]

For how long is material to be preserved: the issue of time
The time factor is a neglected aspect of preservation policy. There is an underlying assumption in much of the literature that there is a stark and simple contrast between no preservation at all and permanent retention. This is neither true nor particularly logical. In practice, the utility of library materials is determined in part by their age, just as it is in part by their subject matter. It has already been suggested that yesterday's newspapers are of little interest to a public library. Even this apparently obvious statement needs some qualification. Most public libraries, for example, consider it their duty to preserve a complete run of newspapers published in their own locality. In that respect, they take

on the archival function of a research library, and therefore commit themselves to the preservation of information and of materials. Newspaper cuttings on specific subjects are an important part of the information resource in many special libraries. Such cuttings are assumed to have some value beyond the date of publication of the newspaper. How long will they be kept? And what measures will be needed to ensure that they are usable for the whole of that time?

Specific questions of this kind can be asked about many categories of material. Is it the policy to retain annual reference books when the next year's volume is published? If so, why is this done? What level of use is expected? Will they be held on open access or in closed storage areas? All of these factors will affect preservation decisions. To put the matter at its crudest, if the covers come away from *Who's who* in November, and it will be discarded when the new volume is published in January, what is the point of anything other than simple palliative measures to keep the book in usable condition for a few more weeks? If it is intended to preserve it after that time, it may indeed be necessary to repair it properly, but if it is to be discarded the expenditure cannot be justified.

One particular category of material can be highlighted to permit a further exploration of this dilemma. It is well known that research scientists rely very heavily on journal literature, but that papers are most frequently consulted very soon shortly after publication. Thereafter, consultation is infrequent, and in some disciplines almost unknown. The phenomenon known as 'citation decay' sets in at a fairly early stage in a paper's life. Moreover, although the rate of decay does indeed vary between different branches of science, the principle is universal. Bibliometric studies have shown that the 'half-life' of a scientific paper (i.e., its generally useful lifetime) may be as little as four to five years, after which it is rarely cited.[11]

These considerations are fundamental to managing the preservation of scientific journals. If the working life of a journal is five years, for example, is it possible to justify the cost of binding it? Indeed, the process of binding may actually reduce the utility of the journal, since it will be out of use for at least a few days, and more often several weeks, while it is being bound. This will typically be some three to twelve months after publication. Yet this is the height of its useful life, when the papers it contains are beginning to be listed in annual indexes and abstracts and the demand for them consequently increases. The supposed conflict between preservation and use barely exists in such cases. Provided that a five-year working life can be assured in other ways, binding cannot be justified even in terms of the use of the materials, let alone in economic terms. Other questions arise for such journals. When the half-life of the journal has been reached, is there a case for disposal? Shelf-space is expensive, and long runs of periodicals can occupy far more of it than their use justifies. For many scientific libraries, currency is far more important than archiving, and the permanent preservation of material which might one day be of historical interest is more properly left to others.

By what means is it to be preserved: the issue of methods
The decision to preserve individual items, or whole classes of materials, can only be implemented if a means of preservation is available. The basic choice which has to be made is to determine whether it is the book or the information which is the priority for preservation. In most cases, of course, preserving the book (or manuscript or other medium) will preserve the information which it carries, although very occasionally it may be that in order to ensure its physical survival, consultation can take place only under very carefully controlled circumstances. Such a solution has been adopted for major manuscripts and documents such as The Book of Kells and Domesday Book, where scholars normally consult facsimiles or other reproductions rather than the original. In most cases, of course, some less radical means will be used. If there is not an overwhelming case for the preservation in pristine form of the original document, the normal practice is to take active steps to preserve it only if it can subsequently be used in a reasonable way. This may mean anything from full-scale rebinding to minor repairs. It may also mean – and this is one of the options most frequently chosen – the use of 'temporary' measures such as storing items in boxes, folders and the like to protect them from further damage. Such measures are cheap and simple, and perhaps especially commend themselves to large libraries with major problems and comparatively limited budgets.

The extreme alternative to the preservation of books is the preservation of information, by copying the information into some other medium which is more durable or more easily replicated. In practice, this normally means making archival-standard microfilms. The master negative is copied immediately after processing, and it is from the copy, or *internegative*, that all subsequent copies are made. The master is held in secure storage against the need to make another internegative at some time in the future. From the internegative it is possible to make positive films for use or sale, and prints if these are needed. Film has the advantage of preserving everything about the original except its format, so that the reader can see the text as it was originally presented. No editorial work is involved, and the possibility of error is comparatively slight. The creation of such surrogates has become a major instrument of preservation in both the United States and Europe, and as the extent of the preservation problem is revealed it is becoming ever more attractive as a solution to an otherwise insoluble problem.[12]

Making the choices

The basic decisions about preservation policy ultimately depend upon the answers given, whether locally, regionally or nationally, to the questions which we have suggested. Such a policy, preferably embodied in a document available to all relevant personnel in the library, cannot determine decisions, but it can help to determine the limits within which individual decisions are to be taken. These may be about particular books or documents, or whole classes of material defined by age, subject, use or other agreed criteria. In special cases, reference to the policy document is the ultimate justification for the conclusion which is reached. It ensures a reasonable degree of consistency, not merely of preservation activities, but in ensuring that such activities are within the overall objectives of the library or archive.

A number of complex typologies of preservation decision-making have been suggested,[13] and in a simplified form such typologies are not unhelpful. The schemes proposed in Table 1 below relate use and

Table 1 Preservation options

Use	Priority	Action
High	High	Preserve or replace
Moderate	High	Preserve or replace
Low	High	Preserve
High	Moderate	Preserve or replace
Moderate	Moderate	Preserve
Low	Moderate	Preserve or substitute
High	Low	Preserve
Moderate	Low	Substitute or dispose
Low	Low	Dispose

priority to the action to be taken.[14] The terms 'high', 'moderate' and 'low' can only be very generally defined, although circulation statistics, local surveys of use and so on may help to assign specific numerical values. 'Priority' is ultimately a matter of judgement, although here also help can be sought from the general collection development policy and perhaps from the results of a Conspectus survey. Despite the need for specific institutional definitions, however, the essential relationships can be generalized. A few examples may help to illustrate both the utility and the limitations of such an approach.

As a first example, and incidentally to illustrate the pervasiveness of preservation in so many aspects of librarianship, let us consider a popular novel in the lending stock of a public library. Clearly this is in the 'high use' category, but would not normally be regarded as a high priority *for preservation*. On the other hand, there are other considerations to be taken into account in defining 'priority', especially if we follow the practice of one leading expert and substitute the term 'value', which he takes 'to include bibliographic, aesthetic and financial factors'.[15]

If the library's policy is to retain such fiction in the general lending stock for, say, five years and if that is expected to generate, say, 200 loans, then its preservation for that time, in a condition which permits that level of use, is indeed a high priority. It therefore falls into the high use/high priority category, which effectively dictates permanent availability either by preservation or by replacement. As the book reaches the end of its desired life, however, it changes category. Towards the end of the five-year period it has probably reached the moderate use/moderate priority category, and replacement is less likely to be considered. If it is earmarked for disposal at the end of its life, 'preservation' at this stage may take the form of little more than running repairs carried out by unskilled junior staff. If, on the other hand, it is destined to be sent to a reserve store for more or less permanent retention, then more active steps may be needed at the time of its relegation to ensure its continued survival in a usable condition. This might suggest the low use/moderate priority level of action.

Just as public libraries are sometimes assumed, even by their own managers, not to be involved in preservation activities,[16] so it is commonly thought that research libraries seek to preserve everything. Both assumptions are fallacious. In practice, most materials in research libraries fall into the low use category. Those which do not are, in general, reference materials of the kind which are heavily used and readily available in many libraries. Nevertheless, even low use materials, if they are important as research materials, have to be preserved in some form. Replacement by acquiring another copy is, generally speaking, very difficult; and if older books are involved, as they often are, this may entail high direct and indirect costs in locating and purchasing a copy. In the case of unique items, which, by definition, includes all manuscript documents, replacement is of course impossible. The low use/low priority category is effectively excluded from consideration in such a library since disposal is not normally an acceptable course of action for material of this kind. In practice, the choice is between preservation or substitution on the one hand, and the creation of a surrogate followed by minimal passive measures to preserve the original on the other.[17] Newspapers, in particular, because they are so difficult to preserve and to store (and generally in very poor condition), have been the main priority for surrogate creation programmes in Britain and many other countries until recently. They could be argued to fall into the low use/moderate priority category suggested here, leaving the low use/high priority ranking for those items for which a surrogate is not acceptable because the book or document is itself an historic object. However, there are no easy answers, and even major research libraries are beginning to reconsider their commitment to total preservation.

It should always be remembered that the objective of a preservation policy is to make information available to users by selecting for preservation the material in which information is stored. It is neither desirable nor possible to preserve everything. Even national libraries have to be selective; a recent proposal from the British Library suggests that selectivity will become an even more significant element of collection management and preservation policies in that institution.[18] The pressures for selectivity, however, both there and elsewhere, are not only financial or space-related. There are sound professional and intellectual reasons for relating the size and quality of the stock to the demands and needs of the users, and doing so with a proper consideration of information resources which are available from elsewhere. National policies for preservation, like national policies for information development in general, are the context in which local and institutional decisions have to be taken. It has been forcefully argued that the availability of high-quality interlending services can assist not only in providing rapid access to information, but also in preserving the information itself.[19] The sharing of resources was the starting-point for the evolution of the Conspectus concept, and has become the driving force behind a number of important preservation initiatives, especially in the high-cost area of surrogate creation.[20] We shall return to this in Chapter Seven, for inter-institutional co-operation, local, national and international, is a key area of preservation policy implementation.

References

1 Gwinn, N. E. and Mosher, P. H., 'Coordinating collection development: the RLG Conspectus', *College and research libraries*, **44**, 1983, 128 – 40.

2 Stam, D. H., 'Collaborative collection development: progress, problems, and potential', *IFLA journal*, **12**, 1986, 9 – 19.

3 Holt, B. G. F. and Hanger, S., *Conspectus in the British Library: a summary of current collecting intensity data as recorded on RLG conspectus worksheets with completed worksheets on microfiche*, London, The British Library, 1986; and Hanger, S., 'Collection development in the British Library: the role of the RLG Conspectus', *Journal of librarianship*, **19**, 1987, 89 – 107.

4 Matheson, A., 'The planning and implementation of Conspectus in Scotland', *Journal of librarianship*, **19**, 1987, 141 – 51.

5 Schmidt, J. and Ventress, A., *Draft collection development policy*, Sydney, State Library of New South Wales, 1988, 14 – 24, 33 – 158. I am grateful to Ms Janine Schmidt, the Library's Director of Collection Services, for giving me a copy of this document.

6 Naylor, B., 'Conservation and Conspectus', in National Preservation Office, *Conservation and collection management*, London, The British Library (National Preservation Office Seminar Paper, 2), 1988, 26. For an example of Conspectus being used in a preservation programme, see Walker, G., 'Advanced preservation planning at Yale', *Microform review*, **18**, 1989, 20 – 8.

7 Smethurst, J. M., 'The relationship between acquisition, retention and preservation policies', in National Preservation Office, *Conservation and collection management*, 11 – 19.

8 Tominger, C., 'Selecting library materials for preservation', *Library and archival security*, **7**, 1985, 1 – 6.

9 Bagnall, R. S. and Harris, C. L., 'Involving the scholars in preservation decisions: the case of the classicists', *Journal of academic librarianship*, **13**, 1987, 140 – 6.

10 Enright, B., Hellinga, L. and Leigh, B., *Selection for survival. A review of acquisition and retention policies*, London, The British Library, 1989, 5 – 6, 32 – 4, 37.

11 Meadows, A. J., *Communication in science*, London, Butterworths, 1974, 126 – 51. See also below, 79–80.

12 For a general study, see Gwinn, N. E. (ed.), *Preservation microfilming. A guide for librarians and archivists*, Chicago, Ill., London, American Library Association, 1987.

13 For two examples, see Atkinson, R. W., 'Selection for preservation: a materialistic approach', *Library resources and technical services*, **30**, 1986, 341 – 53; and Child, M. S., 'Further thoughts on "Selection for preservation: a materialistic approach"', *Library resources and technical services*, **30**, 1986, 354 – 62.

14 For a similar scheme, see Clements, D.W.G., 'Policy planning in the U.K.: from local to national', in Palmer, *Preserving the word*, 25.

15 By Clements, 'Policy planning', in Palmer, *Preserving the word*. I accept this definition *provided that* 'bibliographic' is generously interpreted to mean more than merely physical characteristics, and 'value' also means 'significance in the context of this collection', i.e. 'priority'.

16 Liddle, D., 'Conservation: the public library view', in National Preservation Office, *Conservation and collection management*, 29 – 38.

17 See the draft policy statement on 'The retention or disposal of newspapers after microfilming', produced by the IFLA Working Group on Newspapers, and printed in Gibb, I.(ed.), *Newspaper preservation and access* (Symposium held in London, 12 – 15 August 1987), 2 vols, Munich, New York, London, Paris, K.G. Saur (IFLA Publications, 45, 46), 1988, vol. 2, 421 – 3.

18 Enright, Hellinga and Leigh, *Selection for survival*, 32 – 4, 41 – 2.

19 Line, M. B., 'Interlending and conservation: friends or foes?', *Interlending and document supply*, **16**, 1988, 7 –11.

20 Govan, J. F., 'Preservation and resource sharing: conflicting or complementary?', *IFLA journal*, **12**, 1986, 20 – 4.

5 *The physical dimension of preservation*

An understanding of the use of books and information, both generally and in a particular library, is the necessary foundation of a preservation policy. Before that policy can be fully implemented, however, there is another set of factors which needs to be considered. Preservation policy makes sense only if it is technically and economically realistic, so that until a library or archive knows the extent of its own preservation needs it cannot usefully determine what its policy shall be. As we have seen, the preservation problem arises from two fundamental physical causes: first, there are the inherent properties and weaknesses of the materials used as information media; and secondly, we must consider the interaction between the materials and the environment in which they are stored and used. In developing a policy, therefore, both the materials and the building have to be systematically surveyed. The objective of the survey is to find out about existing conditions and to try to discern possible future difficulties.

Surveying the building

The preservation survey logically starts with the building, since that contains the environment in which most library and archive materials spend almost all of their time. It should always be remembered that, with the exception of the most heavily used items in the loan stock, library materials spend virtually their entire life not merely in the building, but actually on the shelf. It is there, *in situ*, that deterioration starts; preservation has to follow its example. It is important to maintain a clear distinction between a preservation survey of a building and the sort of survey which might be undertaken by an architect or an engineer. The preservation survey is a matter for a professional librarian or archivist, aware of the professional issues which arise from the conditions in which materials are stored. The basic environmental hazards to library materials – temperature, humidity, light, air quality and biological pests – dictate the form of the survey, which will seek to discover and evaluate both natural and man-made hazards.

The starting-point is the general condition of the building as a whole. The concern is not so much to discover serious structural or material defects, but rather to assess the general suitability of the building for its purpose. The materials that are used – wood, brick or stone, for example – will affect weatherproofing and heat insulation. A flat roof can lead to difficulties with water seepage in heavy rain. Ill-fitting doors and windows can admit both water and animal life. These are basic facts with which the librarian has to live. Since they can only be changed by costly structural alterations, it is particularly important to be aware of them.[1]

Inside the building, the survey will look at matters which are perhaps rather more under the control of the librarian. Above all, it is necessary to know the humidity and temperature of storage areas; this is of course critical in areas used for housing materials of exceptional value, importance or fragility, or very valuable materials such as film. The preservation survey will note by what systems the building is heated, cooled and ventilated, how the systems are actually used, and how effective they are. For example, if air-conditioning systems are turned off at weekends to save money, the temperature may rise to unacceptable levels. In library and archive buildings which do not have full environmental control systems, which are probably the majority, there are usually seasonal variations in temperature and humidity. This is especially true in those parts of the world where there are significant seasonal changes in the weather, such as a north European winter or a tropical rainy season. The initial survey, therefore, has to be carried out over a period of at least one year, and also has to take into account any freak condition in that year, such as an unusually harsh winter or an exceptionally hot summer.

The means and intensity of lighting also have to be noted, as does the incidence of direct sunlight in storage areas. Finally, the survey will have an assessment, necessarily subjective, of the general cleanliness and tidiness of the storage areas, and there will be an inspection for any signs of animal droppings which might indicate infestation of the building by rodents or other pests. Special areas within the building, such as those used for exhibitions, will be the subject of special inspections.[2]

Even in closed-access non-circulating collections, materials do not spend all their time either on the shelf in the stack or on users' desks. They travel between stacks and reading areas, and may be sent to and from the bindery or the photographic studio. They are received in an accessions area and pass through cataloguing areas. Although the environmental conditions in such places are not of such critical concern as those in storage areas, since the materials are only in fairly short-term transit, it is important that the procedures used for transportation and handling are consistent with the needs of preservation. The design of book trolleys, the size of cataloguers' desks and the areas available for storage of books and manuscripts in a photographic studio are among the many concerns of the preservation survey.

Surveying the collections
The inspection of the building is only the first stage of the initial preservation survey and arguably the less important. There follows the survey of the collections themselves, for whose protection the whole programme is to be designed. Even in a comparatively small library it is normally impossible to inspect every item. Survey techniques have to be used which will examine a statistically valid sample of holdings, so that it is possible to form an acceptably accurate overall impression of the condition and needs of the collection. The precise method will vary according to the size and nature of the institution and its holdings, but the normal pattern would be to examine items selected by using a table of random numbers, ensuring that all parts of the collection and storage areas are sampled in this way. Where the collections can be divided into discrete elements which may have different preservation needs – manuscripts and printed books, for example – each element will be separately subjected to the same technique.

A general preservation survey cannot reveal minute details about every book or document. It merely records fairly generalized impressions of the overall condition of the collections, and so there is, inevitably, an element of subjectivity. It is for this reason that the sampling technique is so important; it is the only truly objective criterion in the survey. The staff who undertake a preservation survey need some basic training; indeed, ideally they will be professional librarians or archivists. The survey will look for signs of damage by excessive or careless use, as well as dirt, water stains and damp, insect infestation, moulds, paper decay or embrittlement and general deterioration of paper and bindings. The normal practice is to record this data on standard forms which can then be collated.[3] It is through such sample surveys that the full extent of the preservation problem in the world's libraries and archives has been gradually revealed.[4]

A general preservation survey of the collections provides the essential data needed for the planning of future action. Particular attention is obviously paid to materials which fall into the high priority category, and if large quantities of such items are found to be in a seriously decayed condition immediate steps will have to be taken.

In a particularly important collection, it may be desirable to inspect the contents item by item. This is very time-consuming; it may well be justified only when a collection has already been identified from the general survey as a priority for active conservation work. In other words, it is high priority material in generally poor condition which is treated in this way. Indeed, a detailed survey has to be conducted before conservation work can be effectively organized. When individual books, manuscripts or documents are being inspected more details can be recorded than for entire collections, and there will, of course, be more specific statements about condition and proposed treatment. There are even some particular tests which can be carried out if the importance and general state of the material is considered to justify this.

Before planning such a survey, it is important to define its objective. In particular, if it has already been decided that the collection is to be preserved in the original format, then the conservation survey will be directed towards determining the appropriate repair or restoration work to be undertaken on each book. If, on the other hand, it has been agreed that surrogates are acceptable if they are necessary, or that replacement is suitable if it is possible, then the designation of which items can be repaired and which will have to be substituted is a high priority in the survey itself. In such a case the actual details of the work to be undertaken need be specified only for those items on which conservation work is thought to be desirable.

A possible model for a book report form for a conservation survey can be found in Figure 6.[5] There will, of course, be local variations according to the nature of the collection, the funding available for the survey (and indeed for subsequent conservation work) and the skill and knowledge of the staff available to undertake the survey. In essence, however, this form records all that needs to be known at this stage.

CONSERVATION SURVEY

BOOK REPORT FORM

SHELF-MARK........ DATE OF REPORT.........NAME.........

		Condition	Work needed
BINDING:	Hinges		
	Boards		
	Spine		
	Cover		
	Sewing		
PAPER:	pH level		
	Embrittled		
	Mould		
	Insect damage		
	Water damage		
	Fire/heat damage		
	Mutilated		
	Annotations		

Fig. 6 Conservation survey: book report form

Much of what is recorded may seem to be a little vague but if the staff are given clear instructions, this is not a major problem. For example, if a distinction is to be maintained between 'broken' hinges, meaning that the board is detached, and 'weak' hinges, meaning that the board is still attached but in danger of coming away, that can be fully explained and then consistently applied. It requires no great technical knowledge, and the terminology is unambiguous.

Two items on the form are more specific, and call for further explanation. Both relate to the discovery of a high level of acid in the paper. The measurement of the pH level requires the use of the appropriate instrument, a pH meter, which records the relative proportions of acid and alkali in the paper. Such instruments are available from all conservation supply firms, and are easy to use. The measurement of embrittlement is a different and slightly more controversial matter. One measure which is often applied is the so-called 'fold test'. This involves folding the corner of a leaf backwards and forwards along the same line until it breaks. As a general rule, paper is considered to be embrittled if this break takes place after six or fewer folds. Obviously, if a book is discovered to be embrittled, then it suffers further damage when the paper breaks during this test; even if it is not, the leaf chosen for testing is weakened. The fold test is a useful device, but it might be argued that it should be applied sparingly. It is only necessary when embrittlement seems likely to be a major problem. Since it is a consequence of the breakdown of the fibres in acidic paper, other tests of acidity, such as pH measurement, or even simple observation of the browning of the paper, are to be preferred, at least in the first instance. It is also worth remembering that in Britain, so far as we know, embrittlement is not the predominant preservation problem that it now is in the United States.

Using the survey: the building

The purpose of the preservation surveys of the building and its contents is to provide information upon which managerial decisions about policy can be soundly based. In the case of the building, three lines of policy need to be developed:

- a maintenance programme
- security arrangements
- a disaster plan.

Obviously, any properly managed organization which occupies a building for which it is responsible has a maintenance programme. For library and archives buildings, however, there are some special considerations. The internal environment is so important that continuous monitoring is probably desirable, at least in areas in which high priority materials are stored and used. This means monitoring the temperature, humidity and air quality, and then using whatever means are available for regulating them to achieve the desired conditions. The preservation policy will prescribe both the levels to be maintained, and the regularity of the monitoring. It is also important in this as in other aspects of preservation policy that a proper reporting mechanism is established, so that if maintenance staff discover a problem the facts are made known as soon as possible to the librarian or archivist responsible for the preservation management programme. In any case, reports of the readings from the monitoring devices ought to be made available to the manager on a regular basis.

The building survey may have revealed potential hazards in some areas. Those areas need to be particularly carefully monitored. Where materials are stored close to possible sources of water leakage, for example, regular checks are needed to ensure that no such problems have occurred.

The human element in preservation policy can never be ignored, and the building survey may well reveal weak points which might be exploited by the unscrupulous. Damage to books, even by proper use, is caused by people as much as by natural hazards, but most of that is accidental or careless. Occasionally, however, theft or deliberate damage do take place. Neither can wholly be prevented, but adequate and reasonable security arrangements are nevertheless an integral part of the preservation policy. Theft is a danger which cannot be ignored in any library. For research libraries and archives, containing material with a high commercial value, it is especially important to take steps to prevent it, but the need is not confined to them. Security measures may include the vetting of potential users, the guarding of exits by security officers or electronic systems, and the searching or deposit of bags and other containers.[6] The usual anti-theft precautions are either bag-checks or, most commonly today, electronic 'tagging' of books. In such systems, a magnetized strip is inserted invisibly in the book; the strip is desensitized when the item is properly checked out through the circulation system. If it is not desensitized, it sets off an alarm when carried through the electronic gates at the exit. Such systems are not cheap, but they are almost infallible and could be argued to be very cost-effective.

Theft can never be eliminated, but it can be reduced to insignificant proportions. If thefts of valuable or important material do take place, they should be reported to the police, but in both Britain and the United States reporting systems have been developed by librarians and antiquarian booksellers (who also suffer badly from theft) to circulate the details of stolen books and thereby prevent their resale.[7] Serious professional theft for commercial purposes is most likely to be of older and rarer materials. However, perhaps it is worth remembering that many such thefts have been from libraries which have little-used collections of older books. In such circumstances, security is sometimes lax, since that part of the collection is not a high priority. To compound the difficulty, it may be a long time before the theft is actually discovered. Finally, a few very high-profile institutions, especially in politically unstable regions, may also feel that precautions have to be taken against possible acts of terrorism.

Controlling the damage done to materials is much more difficult than theft prevention. Minute supervision of reading areas is impossible in all but the most specialized cases. In a large research library, the main reading room can rarely be supervised in detail; even reading rooms for rare books and manuscripts may be subject to little more than general scrutiny. Lending libraries have a far greater problem, as do those libraries in which continuous supervision of public areas is impossible for architectural or economic reasons. The mutilation of books is all too common in both public and academic libraries. Cursory checks when books are returned from loan reveal the damage, but not the culprit. Exhortation is probably the only practical solution to this problem, and that has obvious limitations.

Avoiding of preventing loss or damage is an important part of any preservation programme. The greatest difficulty arises when the unpredictable happens. It is in this case that the disaster plan becomes central to the preservation strategy. The preparation of a disaster plan (or disaster *preparedness* plan as it is coming to be called, rather less ambiguously) has become a key element in preservation policy-making during the last few years. In Britain, however, it made a slow start. The questionnaire for the Ratcliffe inquiry did not even ask specifically about disaster plans;[8] nor did that for a world-wide survey sponsored by Unesco, IFLA and ICA in 1986.[9] A survey in 1986 revealed that only 6.6% of a large sample of libraries and archives in England, Wales and Northern Ireland had a disaster plan, and only a further 3.7% were engaged in compiling one.[10] The pioneer of disaster planning in the United Kingdom was the National Library of Scotland, whose published version of its knowledge and experience, dating from 1985, remains an invaluable source for all those involved in disaster preparedness.[11] Work began much earlier in the United States. The first significant published guide there dates from as long ago as 1978.[12]

The building survey is the starting-point for the disaster plan, since it reveals the building's inherent hazards from water and fire, the two most likely causes of large-scale disasters in temperate climates. In modern buildings, such hazards abound. They are found in water-based heating and cooling systems, as well as the plumbing of lavatories, drinking water supplies, and so on. Above all, however, we have to look at the vastly complicated electrical systems and installations used for lighting, air-conditioning systems, and the operation of equipment such as lifts, photographic apparatus, binding machinery, microform readers and computers. Certain rooms or areas can also be identified as being particularly hazardous. These include computer rooms, binderies, conservation laboratories, photographic studios, kitchens and any part of the building where smoking is allowed. There may also be temporary hazards created from time to time by building works, and indeed by workmen. At least one major library fire is believed to have been caused by a smouldering cigarette butt dropped by a workman engaged in roof repair work. To some extent, all of these hazards can be anticipated by installing monitoring decvies, such as smoke, heat and fire detectors, and regular monitoring of them. In addition, essential safety regulations relating to electrical apparatus and other potential hazards should be meticulously enforced.

Away from the comparatively benign climatic conditions of north-west Europe, other hazards also need to be taken into account. These include earthquakes, monsoons, hurricanes, forest or bush fires and similar natural occurrences. In general terms, these are predictable. We do not know exactly when they are going to happen, but it is possible to make reasonable estimates of the probability of their happening eventually. Indeed, some of them can be considered at the time when the building is being designed. In some parts of the world, for example, building regulations prescribe the maximum height and minimum strength of buildings erected in earthquake zones. Unlike these events, human error or malice cannot be predicted. Arson has been the cause of a number of major library fires in recent years.[13] Although disaster *prevention* is the best remedy, disaster *preparedness* is the best response to the unpredictable and the unpreventable.

The disaster plan essentially dictates what shall be done, and just as importantly who shall be responsible for doing it, if a disaster occurs. The general pattern is to assign responsibility for the design and execution of the plan to a senior member of the library staff, and then to establish a committee which develops and implements the plan. An important element in the implementation stage is staff training, so that everyone knows what to do if disaster strikes. It should be remembered that disasters are not confined to working hours, and out-of-hours contacts and telephone numbers are a key element of the plan. So too is liaison with local emergency services, and especially with the fire brigade who are the first line of defence against both fire and flood. It has to be recognized, of course, that if a fire breaks out when the building is occupied, evacuation is the first priority. The means of achieving this are also a part of the disaster planning process. Indeed, regular, but unannounced, fire drills are invaluable both as a test of the evacuation procedures and as a form of staff training.

If a disaster should occur, nothing can be done until the immediate crisis is passed, especially in the case of fire. It is the next stage which is critical to the rescue and survival of books and documents. Water damage is both the most insidious and the most likely consequence of any disaster. Immediate drying of sodden materials is essential if they are to have any chance of survival and for this industrial-scale deep-freezing is necessary. Part of the disaster planning process is to discover where such facilities are available, and to make contingency plans for their use in an emergency. Fire-damaged materials are even more difficult to rehabilitate than water-damaged items, and specialist advice will have to be sought. The disaster plan will include the names of such specialists as well as lists of organizations, individuals and companies which will be needed during the rescue and recovery period.[14]

Using the survey: the collections

The survey of the collections as a whole, and of individual items within them, is intended to reveal the need for preservation and conservation. This is then related to the broader priorities established by other means. The preservation policy defines the general outlines of the actions which are to be taken in regard to damaged or endangered items, in particular in two areas:

- binding and repair work
- reformatting for information preservation.

Where it is considered that damaged items have to be kept in their original physical format, binding and repair work, both restorative and preventative, will need to be undertaken. The range of options available is wide; which option is adopted for a particular book will be determined by a number of factors including the cost of the treatment, the significance of the book itself and the use to which it is likely to be subject.[15] For recently acquired materials, some preventative work may be justified before it is even added to stock, if it will lengthen its useful life. The widespread practice of strengthening paperbacks is one well-known example. The regular binding of completed volumes of

71

periodicals is also a common practice, and is certainly justified where a high use periodical is expected to continue to be in demand for some time after publication. Individual decisions on such matters are most effectively taken within the broad guidelines of an agreed policy, and will be discussed at length in Chapter Six.

The preservation or conservation of older materials presents more complex issues. In some cases, it may be desirable to transfer materials from general to special collections if they will then be housed in more suitable conditions.[16] Repairs should not be undertaken at random, but within broad policy guidelines. For high priority/high use material of no particular historical importance, any repair will take the form of using the strongest bindings available. Books which are of historical significance have to be repaired by craftsmen using appropriate materials; the preservation policy lays down the conditions under which such repairs can be undertaken, and the limits of permissible work. Where full repair is not justified, but it is desirable to keep the item in its original format, some temporary preventative measure may be possible. Such measures include portfolios, boxes and folders, or even different storage systems, such as flat storage of bound volumes of newspapers, or large drawers for the storage of unfolded maps or prints. For non-paper materials, such as film or tapes, appropriate cabinets can be provided.[17]

If preservation in the original format is considered to be undesirable, unnecessary or impossible, then a policy for reformatting for information preservation will be needed. The choice of format is critical. It is determined by a combination of such factors as cost, availability of equipment both for copying and for consultation, acceptability of the surrogate format to readers and, of course, the survival properties of the surrogate format itself. In practice, almost all surrogate creation in libraries and archives has been on microform. The use of 35-mm microfilm probably predominates in in-house projects, but microfiche is preferred by many commercial publishers. In technical terms, microform surrogate programmes present no very serious problems. Well-established standards exist for photography, processing and storage of film.[18] In practice, the great obstacle is finance, for the costs are high; a study in the United States in 1984 – 6 showed a median cost of US$31.91 per title for filming alone, even in a major project in which some economies of scale could be achieved; to this has to be added the associated administrative costs.[19]

Format conversion is normally undertaken for a substantial body of material rather than for individual items. The preservation policy is unlikely to do much more than to indicate that the institution regards format conversion as an acceptable preservation option in certain circumstances, and to indicate circumstances and the preferred surrogate format. The detailed selection of materials will probably present few problems, since whole categories of material will be involved – newspapers are perhaps the most common and obvious example – rather than individual items on which individual decisions are needed.

Conclusion

The development of an agreed preservation policy is perhaps the most important step forward which a library can take in making preservation a part of its normal management procedures. The policy has to be defined and agreed at the highest level in the institution, and command the general support of all those who will be involved with it. To be acceptable, it has to be based on the true needs of the institution. Some libraries may feel justified in preserving nothing, but even that decision has to be based on a proper consideration of the available information and of the implications of the decision. A policy to preserve everything, such as was alleged to exist in so many British libraries in the early 1980s, has even more significant implications which need to be understood. By considering the use, environment and physical condition of the collections, library managers will learn a great deal about the institutions which are in their care. Much of what is learned has implications far beyond the simplistic understanding (or rather misunderstanding) of preservation as being 'something to do with binding'. It impinges on library activities at every point from acquisition to disposal; it affects bibliographic record-keeping; it affects use; it affects policies relating to security, loans and users; it affects the design and maintenance of the building itself. Preservation is essential to the proper management of the library's most important material resource: its collection of media in which the information sought by its users is stored. The management of the preservation programme – the implementation of an agreed policy – is therefore one of the most important professional activities of the librarian or archivist.

References

1 Cunha, G. M., Lowell, H. P. and Schnare, R. E., Jr, *Conservation survey manual*, New York, New York Library Association, 1982, 14 – 15.

2 Cunha, Lowell and Schnare, *Conservation survey manual*, 17; and Cunha, G. M., *Methods to determine the preservation needs in libraries and archives: a RAMP study with guidelines*, Paris, Unesco (PGI-88/WS/160), 1988, 18 – 20.

3 For such forms, see Cunha, Lowell and Schnare, *Conservation survey manual*, 27; and Cunha, *Methods to determine preservation needs*, 74.

4 For an example, see Bond, R., DeCarlo, M., Henes, E. and Snyder, E., 'Preservation study at the Syracuse University Libraries', *College and research libraries*, **48**, 1987, 132 – 47.

5 For a rather different form, see Cunha, *Methods to determine preservation needs*, 75.

6 Thomas, D., *Study on control of security and storage of holdings: a RAMP study with guidelines*, Paris, Unesco (PGI-86/WS/23), 1987, 19, 24 and the references cited there.

7 See 'Security', *Rare books newsletter*, **34**, November 1989, 30 – 2.

8 Ratcliffe, *Preservation policies*, 76 – 8.

9 Clements, D. W. G., *Preservation and conservation of library documents: a Unesco/IFLA/ICA enquiry into the current state of the world's patrimony*, Paris, Unesco (PGI-87/WS/15), 1987, Annexe 1.

10 Tregarthen, Jenkin I., *Disaster planning and preparedness: an outline disaster control plan*, London, The British Library (BL Information Guides, 5), 1987, 2.

11 National Library of Scotland, *Planning manual for disaster control in Scottish libraries and record offices*, Edinburgh, National Library of Scotland, 1985.

12 Bohem, H., *Disaster prevention and disaster preparedness*, Berkeley, Calif., University of California Press, 1978.

13 Buchanan, S. A., *Disaster planning: preparedness and recovery for libraries and archives*, Paris, Unesco (PGI-88/WS/6), 1988, 2 – 3.

14 Buchanan, *Disaster planning*, 8 – 24, 57 – 87; Tregarthen, Jenkin, *Disaster planning*, 11 – 31, 38 – 48. For British librarians and archivists, Tregarthen Jenkins's Appendix B, 'Useful organisations and institutions' is indispensable.

15 Clements, D. W. G., 'Preservation in original format: policies and options', in Smith, *Preservation of library materials*, vol. 1, 43 – 8.

16 Streit, S. A., 'Transfer of materials from general stacks to special collections', *Collection management*, **7**, 1985, 33 – 46.

17 Kovacs, B., 'Preservation of materials in science and technology libraries', *Science and technology libraries*, **7**, 1987, 3 – 13, is of more general interest than its title might suggest on this aspect of the subject.

18 Roper, M., 'Policy for format conversion: choosing a format', in Smith, *Preservation of library materials*, vol. 1, 59 – 67.

19 McClung, P. A., 'Costs associated with preservation microfilming: results of the Research Libraries Group study', *Library resources and technical services*, **30**, 1986, 363 – 74. But see also 86 – 7, below.

6 *The management of preservation*

The implementation of preservation policies depends, like any other aspect of management, upon the effective deployment of human, material and financial resources to meet agreed common objectives. In essence, a preservation policy defines what is to be preserved, and what methods are to be employed in the preservation of particular classes of materials. It does so, however, in the context of the overall management and development of the collection, and of the conditions in which it is stored and used, as well as in relation to the availability of comparable information resources outside the institution. As an aspect of collection management, preservation is part of that continuous sequence of processes which begins with selection and ends with withdrawal or permanent retention. At a more mundane level, however, the implementation of policy-level preservation decisions depends upon the efficient administration of technical activities such as binding, repair and reprography. Finally, but of great importance, there is the human dimension which is integral to all management; in this case, that means the need for committed and properly trained staff at all levels.

Policy implementation
The implementation of general policies to particular cases depends upon a knowledge and understanding of the policy itself and of the context in which it has been developed. The point is perhaps best illustrated by some examples of groups of materials which present particular preservation problems.

The first category, and one which is exceptionally troublesome for the preservation manager, is that of *newspapers*. Newspapers are, by definition, ephemeral. A newspaper, with rare exceptions such as the so-called (and usually self-styled) 'newspapers of record', are documents intended to be read once by two or three people and then thrown away. Preservation by libraries and archives is a very minor objective for most newspaper producers. Newspapers are published, printed and distributed under conditions in which the significant factors are speed and cheapness. The newspaper industry, since its emergence in the seventeenth and eighteenth centuries, has always been highly competitive, but it has only rarely experienced periods of financial or organizational stability. In Britain alone, there have been tens of thousands of newspaper titles published since the early seventeenth century, some of them continuing for tens of thousands of issues. Each issue was printed in numbers ranging from a few hundreds, in the early days, to the several millions of daily copies which typify the present-day tabloids. Every country with a free press shows a similar pattern of newspaper development, and has a similarly large output; even in countries where press freedom is limited, the output of newspapers is generally on a large scale because of their usefulness as instruments of state propaganda. In recent years, historians have increasingly recognized the value of newspapers as historical sources, while modern methods of indexing have made possible the more effective retrieval of the huge quantities of information which they contain. Demand for them by users of research collections, and especially of historical collections, is consequently increasing.

The preservation of newspapers presents two related physical problems: there are huge numbers of them, and they are generally printed on very poor paper.[1] It is these two factors which have determined the direction of newspaper preservation in recent years. The sheer scale of the problem made it inevitable that newspapers would be among the first groups of material to be the subject of mass microfilming programmes for preservation purposes. Indeed, there was a secondary advantage, in addition to the need to transfer the information to a more durable medium. Few libraries hold complete runs of early newspapers, and the preservation microfilms, by drawing on the resources of a number of institutions, were more complete than the holdings of any individual library. Needless to say, large-scale microfilming of newspapers calls for large-scale capital investment. This has been a serious obstacle to more projects being undertaken, despite the fact that such projects are generally considered to be desirable.[2] It should be added, however, that there is sufficient demand for newspapers for the films to be a viable commercial proposition. A considerable number of newspapers have been filmed either by commercial firms, or in collaborative ventures between companies and libraries. A few newspapers, including *The times*, *The New York times* and *Le monde*, and a few magazines, such as *New scientist* and *The spectator*, are even produced in microform by their own publishers at regular intervals for preservation purposes.

The technical decisions involved in a newspaper microfilming programme are comparatively straightforward. Standards exist for archival microfilms, and these are, of course, the standards to which films should be made.[3] In addition, there are some generally accepted requirements which are specific to the filming of newspapers. These include the making of minor repairs before filming, so that crumpled and folded pages, for example, are opened out and flattened, and missing issues are checked and noted. This is in addition to such normal practices as ensuring that materials are carefully handled, leader film is provided, the reduction ratio is clearly stated, and the end-product is checked against the original before any copies are made from the master negative.[4] These are normal precautions, and can be undertaken by any commercial microfilming bureau, of which a number exist. The most difficult and most significant decision is whether the filming should be undertaken in-house or by a commercial bureau. This will depend upon cost estimates, as well as the availability of staff and equipment. In any case, financial resources will almost certainly determine the size and scope of a newspaper microfilming programme. Commercial prices vary, but 1988 costings suggest rates of between £25 and £40 per 100-foot reel of master negative.[5]

The preservation of newspapers is not a matter for research libraries alone. Both in Britain and elsewhere, local and regional newspapers are often found in the public library in their place of publication and sometimes nowhere else. Similarly, incomplete runs in major libraries may be supplemented by copies found in local collections in libraries, record offices and even the newspaper offices themselves. Two examples may serve to illustrate this point. The very important *Northampton mercury*, founded in 1720 and still published, exists in a complete run only in the Local Studies Department at the Central Library in Northampton; there are significant gaps in the holdings of the British Library and of other major libraries. The Northampton run of this newspaper was filmed, by a commercial firm, in 1960.[6] Another example, not quite so venerable but still of importance, is that of the *Berwick advertiser*. The British Library holdings are complete from 1825, when publication began, to the present day, save for the year 1898 and two months in 1912. These gaps can be filled only from the run (also incomplete) held by the publisher, Tweeddale Press of Berwick-upon-Tweed. That run has been filmed for the Northumberland County Record Office by a local microfilm bureau, but the quality of the film is said to be poor.[7] The need to know where newspapers are to be found, and to ensure that archival copies are indeed of an archival standard, is a matter of concern to everyone involved, and is an issue which could arise in any public library or county record office.

The second category of material which helps to exemplify some of the practical questions involved in preservation management is *periodicals*, and in particular the learned and scientific journals to be found in academic libraries. Cost is still a key factor, of course, but so too is time. The typical learned journal is published in parts, with a predetermined number of parts, varying from two to twelve, forming a numbered volume. That volume, usually annual, is normally taken as the unit for binding. It follows therefore that the first part of any given volume will be published up to a whole year before the volume can be bound. By that time, many scientific journals, in particular, will already have been subjected to heavy use, and perhaps to the maximum, or only, use which they are ever likely to have.

The traditional approach to this problem was to regard the most heavily used materials as the priorities for binding, and to ensure that they were bound as quickly as possible after the publication of the volume was complete. This is successful enough in the context of a specialized scientific collection, although it may not be more generally applicable.[8] There is, however, an alternative point of view. If a volume of a journal of immediate, but comparatively short-term, interest is sent away for binding as soon as it is completed by the publication of its final part, that part will be unavailable to users during precisely the period of time when it is in heaviest demand. In science, medicine and engineering this point is particularly relevant. It may well be that, from the user's standpoint, the availability of unbound parts is far more important than their long-term preservation. This is a perfectly legitimate view, and save in research libraries seeking to retain long runs for permanent reference, it need not be a matter of too great concern.

Deciding what materials to send for binding, and the order of priority, will ultimately be a question which is answered in relation to use and resources. A simple but useful model, similar to that suggested in Chapter 5, can express this relationship, and will be found in Table 2 on p.80.[9] In general, the greater the *number of issues per volume*, the higher the priority for binding when the publication of the volume is complete. This is partly dictated by publishing conventions, since the more frequent publications tend to be in larger formats which are less

Table 2   Criteria for the binding of periodicals

Parts/Volume	Use	Lifespan	Priority
< 4	High	> 5 yr	High
< 4	Low	> 5 yr	Medium
5 – 12	High	> 5 yr	High
5 – 12	Low	> 5 yr	Medium
> 12	High	> 5 yr	High
> 12	Low	> 5 yr	Medium
< 4	High	2 – 5 yrs	Medium
< 4	Low	2 – 5 yrs	Low
5 – 12	High	2 – 5 yrs	High
5 – 12	Low	2 – 5 yrs	Medium
> 12	High	2 – 5 yrs	High
> 12	Low	2 – 5 yrs	Medium
< 4	High	< 2 yr	Low
< 4	Low	< 2 yr	Low
5 – 12	High	< 2 yr	Medium
5 – 12	Low	< 2 yr	Low
> 12	High	< 2 yr	Medium
> 12	Low	< 2 yr	Low

easy to store satisfactorily when they are unbound. It is significant, however, that newsletters and letter journals also appear at monthly or even more frequent intervals; these are often of comparatively ephemeral interest at least as far as heavy use is concerned. By contrast, the classic four-part-per-year journal is typically in octavo format, and can be stored in open-topped pamphlet boxes, or, indeed, directly on the shelf. *Frequency of use* is obviously a key factor, but *expected period of currency* is also important. Combining these three factors gives the model suggested in Table 2, in which binding priorities are essentially determined by use, but take account of the physical characteristics of the periodical and its pattern of publication.

A third category of material which illustrates some of the issues in preservation management is that of *paperbacks*. In recent years, public libraries, in particular, have purchased paperbacks in large quantities for two reasons. First, it is felt that they are more attractive to some of the less enthusiastic users of the library, and especially perhaps to children, to whom they are more familiar that the superficially more 'serious' hardback. Secondly, they are of course cheaper. It is the latter factor which is the more important factor for our purposes. If the paperback rather than the hardback edition of a title is selected, this may have several consequences. It may allow more copies of a popular title to be bought, or it may allow more titles to be bought than would otherwise be possible. In times of serious financial restraint, it may even be the only way to maintain a reasonable level and breadth of purchases at all. Whatever the motive (which is in practice likely to be a combination of all of these), the object of the exercise is defeated if the lifespan of the paperback is so short that it has to be replaced, so incurring additional costs, or it is necessary to withdraw it while the title is still in demand.

A recent study of binding methods allows us to suggest some criteria which might be applied to the selection and protection of paperbacks. In general, an 'untreated' paperback, that is a paperback as issued by its publisher, was found to remain in a usable condition for about one year of library use. For popular fiction this would seem to be adequate. The additional expense involved in inserting the books in protective plastic jackets did not significantly improve the situation. Simple reinforcement also had a minimal effect. Only a full case-binding really extended the lifespan of the book, and even that presented some difficulties.[10]

The study was primarily concerned with comparing the properties of various binding styles, and did not really take cost factors into account, although they were, of course, implicit. For the collection manager, however, they are an explicit and crucially important consideration. A typical paperback novel sells at about £2.00, or about 25% of the price of the hardback. Binding may almost double the real cost of the book before it reaches the shelves. In other words, two untreated copies can be replaced in twelve months' time, or four copies can be provided immediately to meet demand, for the same price as one strengthened copy which still has to be replaced at about the same time. The position is different where the price differential is smaller. Non-fiction, or 'trade', paperbacks, which are simply soft-covered reprints of the publisher's hardback edition, are typically priced at between 50% and 65% of the hardback price. Strengthening the binding to make an appreciable difference to its durability may raise the cost to near to the hardback price, and since even a bound paperback never seems to achieve the strength of a hardback, it is probably desirable to buy the hardback in the first place.

A fourth and final issue which illuminates some general points is that of the *transfer of materials* to more protected storage. In most academic and many public libraries, rare books or special collections are housed separately for reasons of security. This separate housing usually means that there is closed-access storage and supervised consultation in a designated reading area, together with restrictions on photocopying, inter-library lending and circulation. Historically, materials for special collections (perhaps the best generic name for this aspect of librarianship) have been selected because of their age or their origin. Thus in many libraries, books printed before a particular date (typically 1800 or 1850) are treated as 'rare' or 'special'. Additionally, collections either assembled or donated *as collections* are usually kept together, often as a tribute to a benefactor.

Generally speaking, it is desirable to transfer into special collections all material in the library which meets the criteria for such a transfer. These criteria are typically:

- *age*, which, as has been suggested, is the principal criterion in most libraries, with 1800 remaining as a popular date, although in terms of rarity and current commercial value 1850 or even 1900 makes as much sense;
- *commercial value*, which may or may not be related to age, is a major criterion, and would be particularly applicable to limited editions, private press books and the like;
- *special factors* may relate to a particular copy, such as provenance or binding, or to the book's importance in a particular library, such as being an example of local printing or relating to some local or regional activity, or being on a subject in which there is a particular collecting interest.

It might be argued that a fourth criterion, condition, should also be applied but, because of the instability of nineteenth- and twentieth-century book materials, this would produce a far higher number of candidates for transfer than would be either feasible or desirable.

Generally speaking, the application of common-sense principles will ensure that transfers reflect the needs of the library and at the same time do not inhibit the use of materials by readers. A more difficult problem is probably posed by the initial identification of material for transfer. In large libraries, systematic searching-out of materials can probably be done only by using those criteria which are searchable in automated catalogues. In practice this would normally mean date of publication, although in particular cases authors, places of publication and subject descriptors might be useful. Serendipity is a very significant factor. When books are returned from loan, or when they are identified during stock checks, for example, they can conveniently be withdrawn from the general to the special collection.[11] It should always be remembered, however, that in selecting material for special collections, the librarian is also redefining the way in which it is used. The closed-access collection is the only solution in some cases, but it has to be accepted that protecting books in this way will make them less accessible to users.[12]

These few examples, are not exhaustive. However, they do help to explain some of the practical dilemmas of preservation policy implementation. Each in its own way illustrates a single point: that there is a symbiosis between preservation policy and user access. A preservation policy which ignores the needs and wishes of potential users of the material is self-defeating. Preservation is a very expensive process. Where users' needs cannot justify the expenditure, as might be argued to be the case in considering the strengthening of paperback fiction, then the money can surely be better spent elsewhere. Even for specialized research materials, access and use are important. With a few exceptions, librarians are not engaged in the preservation of historic artefacts for their own sake, but because they carry words and images whose preservation is desirable. That may be achieved by protecting the book in special collections, or it may be achieved by making a microfilm. It is professional judgement, within broadly agreed policy outlines, which will determine what needs to be done.

Preservation administration

The effective administration of a preservation programme depends upon the joint efforts of library management, junior staff and technicians. The role of the manager is essentially in the determination of policy and its supervision, a role which requires a knowledge of the preservation field, without implying any need to acquire technical skills. This point has often been made, and is now widely accepted in professional circles.[13] Perhaps the one group of exceptions is to be found among some of the more traditional rare book librarians who still seem to regard detailed technical knowledge and even some benchwork skills as an essential part of the librarian's armoury,[14] a view shared to a limited extent by a few educators.[15]

If we leave aside the question of benchwork skills, there are three areas of administrative activity to be considered:

- *the organization of the bindery* and other workshops
- *the determination of the work* to be undertaken and the styles and techniques to be employed
- *the role of all library staff* in ensuring that materials are handled and used in a way which is consistent with their optimal survival.

The *organization of binderies*, photographic studios, conservation laboratories, and the like, is an integral part of the work of the preservation manager. The first stage, however, is to determine whether it is appropriate to have in-house facilities at all. In 1983 – 4, 50 out of 332 British libraries which responded to Ratcliffe's survey had an in-house bindery, 26 a conservation workshop, and 86 some kind of repair facilities. A much higher percentage of academic and research libraries had one or more of these facilities than did libraries in any other group. Far more libraries, however, used external facilities; nearly 300 did so for some purpose or other.[16] It is clear from these statistics that most of the libraries which had in-house facilities also used external binderies when it was considered appropriate. The normal pattern seems to be to use commercial binderies for standard work, such as periodical binding, while undertaking more complex operations in-house. In particular, many libraries prefer to use their own employees and facilities for the repair and conservation of older material, although the British Library has in recent years also used outside binderies for that purpose. Indeed, it has been forcefully argued that there are financial advantages in employing outside organizations or individuals even for high-level conservation work on rare books and manuscripts. There are savings in the indirect costs of employing staff, and it is suggested that the self-employed conservator, working for fees, is likely to maintain a higher rate of productivity than a salaried employee of a library or record office.[17] On the other hand, it has to be remembered that these conservators can and do charge very high fees indeed, in line with the scarcity of their skills and the demand for their services.[18]

Ultimately, such decisions can only be taken at institutional level. As a general rule, however, it will be the larger academic and research libraries which have enough work to keep a bindery fully occupied. For other libraries, the use of commercial binding companies is far more cost-effective, especially when, as in most public libraries, the need is for ordinary work such as periodical binding, paperback strengthening and library-style rebinding of damaged books. Some commercial firms also undertake what they call 'conservation' work. Although some of the specialist conservators dislike the use of the word in this context, and question the quality of some of the work thus produced, the fact is that the commercial binderies are able to undertake work which is adequate for all normal purposes. They can rebind, reback and make boxes, and some can undertake paper repair. Since these are the key areas of conservation work for all but the most valuable material, these companies are quite satisfactory for almost all purposes. In the last analysis, the decision on whether to establish or maintain an in-house bindery is financial. Where resources are very limited, or the work-flow is comparatively small, there is no real option to using outside binderies. In-house facilities are expensive. Moreover, there is a limited supply of skilled persons to work in them, and the commercial binderies are, on the whole, able to offer higher wages than are libraries and record offices. It may be signficant that a book by a distinguished preservation manager, intended as a guide to individuals and small libraries, says nothing about the establishment and administration of the bindery itself. It is, apparently, assumed that any necessary work will be done elsewhere.[19]

The same considerations apply to other preservation facilities. Paper repair and other laboratory activities call for skills which are not widely available, while the facilities themselves occupy a good deal of space. In addition, there are legal requirements in relation to health and safety for the use and storage of chemicals and the use and maintenance of equipment. Traditionally, many record offices have indeed had in-house paper repair and conservation facilities, and continue to do so. In fact, the whole subject of conservation is rightly regarded as a crucial area of the archivist's professional activities and hence an essential part of his or her professional education.[20] Some research libraries have initiated paper-repair laboratories in recent years, especially for their manuscript collections. In general, however, few libraries will wish to move into this field.

The case is, perhaps, slightly different with photographic studios. All libraries have some reprographic capacity, if only for photocopying. Most libraries with research collections also have more sophisticated facilities intended to provide transparencies, 35-mm microfilm, bromide prints and the like, for users. These operations usually work on the expectation of breaking even, and in some cases as profit-making activities. Few in-house studios, however, can cope with large-scale microfilming programmes, although some libraries have established special facilities where surrogate creation has become a principal element in the preservation strategy. The British Library is one such institution,[21] but few libraries would feel able, financially or technically, to follow that example. Again the problem is one of work-flow. Even for quite large-scale substitution programmes, the commercial microfilm bureaux – or better still micropublishers whose sales will help to offset the cost of creating the master negatives and perhaps produce a royalty or fee for the library – are a distinctly preferable option.

Whether the work is undertaken in-house or externally, it will be library staff who *determine what work is actually to be done*. This decision-making process falls essentially into two stages. First, the material to be repaired has to be selected, a subject with which we have already dealt at some length. Secondly, the nature of the work to be undertaken has to be decided, and for this to be done effectively some technical knowledge is indeed essential, so that the librarian understands the options which are available.

Having decided in principle that a particular item or a particular class of material is to be preserved, the next stage is to decide whether preservation is to be in original format or in surrogate form. It has already been suggested that this decision is partly financial, although the nature of the material itself, and its condition, are also factors. Surrogate creation is, in general, very uneconomic for single items such as one book or a small group of documents. The larger the number of uniform items, such as a run of a newspaper, the more economically attractive does surrogacy become, especially if there might be a spin-off in the sale of copies of the microfilm to other libraries. In 1986, it was calculated that the cost of a 35-mm microfilm of a 300-page book was very slightly more than the cost of a made-to-measure box for the same book, and less than one-third of the price of a full-scale rebinding. The figures were £19.50, £18.72 and £67.08 respectively.[22] On this basis, preservation by microfilming might be argued to make sound economic sense even for individual items, but in practice this is rarely true. It is not usual in Britain, although it is in some American libraries, to discard the originals once the master negative has been made. If the book is important enough to film, it is important enough to need more than mere neglect to preserve the original. Hence, in addition to the cost of filming, there will be the cost of the box as well, and perhaps even of significant (and hence expensive) repairs or rebinding. Preservation microfilming generally makes sense only when undertaken on a large scale for a large number of items; this is why a run of a newspaper is so ideal a candidate for such treatment. When programmes are undertaken co-operatively, or as joint ventures with publishers, the costs may be even more favourable to the library.[23]

However, the creation of surrogates is not always the most desirable solution to a preservation problem, even when it is technically feasible and economically viable. Although there are large categories of material for which it is probably the most appropriate option, there will always be a large, and perhaps larger, number of cases in which it is not. In such cases, the choice is essentially between the repair of the damage or the replacement of the item. In many cases, the latter option is not available. Indeed, the scarcity of the item which is considered to be worth preserving will be one factor in determining the priority which it takes in the competition for resources and skills.

In practice, one course of action, or rather inaction, is what has sometimes been called 'benign neglect', that is storage in reasonably good conditions together with the enforcement of high standards of handling and use. For rarely used materials this has been a favoured option in some libraries in recent years, not least because it has the great merit of costing almost nothing. More recently, however, the practice has been challenged from an authoritative source.[24]

If it is decided that some active intervention is needed, this may take the form of repair of the paper (or other material), or, more frequently, of the binding. Paper repair is generally confined to rare and valuable materials, especially manuscripts and archival documents. The one exception is the mass deacidification of embrittled books, although, as we have seen, these processes are still at a comparatively early stage of development. Most conservation work is, in practice, concerned with the repair or replacement of damaged or decayed bindings.

Repair is usually cheaper, although it may not be possible for very badly damaged material. Where the book is of historical interest, and especially if the original binding is significant, it is always desirable to be as conservative as possible in undertaking repairs. It is often possible, for example, to reuse the original boards and their original leather covering, while using new leather for the spine and perhaps resewing the text-block. Original endpapers have to be preserved if they bear, for example, book-plates, other marks of provenance or inscriptions of some kind. Indeed, such endpapers are bound in even if they are no longer functional as endpapers, in order to preserve the historical evidence which they offer. It is often more appropriate to *reback*, that is to repair the existing binding, using as little new material as possible, than it is to *rebind*, that is to remove the remains of the existing binding, and to replace it with a completely new one. It is also almost invariably much cheaper.[25]

However, rebacking and rebinding are not the only options for damaged books. For older books it may be deemed appropriate to use specially made boxes, and these have indeed become an important instrument of preservation in the last ten years. The 'phase' box (so-called because it is, in theory, a temporary expedient) is a made-to-measure box, constructed of acid-free or chemically inert card, designed to protect the book both on the shelf and in transit between the shelf and the reader's desk. It is made of a single piece of card, with a hinged lid, and sometimes with ties to ensure that the book cannot fall out when the box is removed from the shelf. Such boxes are comparatively cheap to make, costing as little as about £10 for one suitable for an eighteenth-century octavo of 200 or so pages.[26] Consequently, large numbers of books can be protected. Boxes may be used either where the book needs protection until the time comes for full-scale repairs (the original 'phase' concept) or because for some reason it may be undesirable to resew or rebind, in order to preserve historical or bibliographical evidence. In practice, of course, these options apply largely to older books or books deemed to be of some permanent historical value. For current materials likely to be of comparatively limited or medium-term interest only, different considerations may apply. These have already been discussed in several contexts, including the issues which arise in considering the preservation of periodicals and paperbacks.[27]

In every case, however, it is essential that the binder has clear instructions from the librarian.[28] The binder will carry out such instructions, but cannot be expected to interpret them or to make deductions about them. It is certainly not the binder's business to guess at what they ought to have been when they are either absent or inadequate. For straightforward work, only straightforward instructions are required. These should specify the general nature of the work to be done, the materials to be used and any special requirements. Thus, for rebinding a recent book, the specification need be no more than 'library binding, blue cloth', together with a note of the words or other matter (such as a shelf-mark), if any, to be embossed on the spine. For periodicals, the instructions are typically a little more complicated, since they have to specify how the parts are to be arranged, whether such material as covers, advertising pages and supplements are to be retained, and if so where they are to be bound in. The instructions will also specify what is to be done about the title-page, index and table of contents, as well as external matters such as the colour of cloth to be used and the wording to be used on the spine. The last two items will be standardized in most libraries, but they do differ from library to library. Many libraries keep standard or specimen bindings in their own binderies which are then imitated year after year to maintain uniformity on the shelves. Commercial binderies have their own specimens, standards and exemplars from which the customer can choose, but they will also create and maintain a design to the customer's own specification.[29] Instructions are normally sent to the bindery in writing, and often on *pro formas* designed for the purpose. In some libraries, the binding records are now automated, and instructions therefore appear in the form of hard-copy print-out from the relevant file. Finally, when completed work is returned from the binder, at least a random sample is normally checked to ensure that the instructions have indeed been followed.

However, preservation is not a matter for specialists alone, or indeed only for professional librarians. It is *the concern of all staff* and all users of a library. A great deal can be achieved in a preservation programme by creating the conditions in which the rate of deterioration of materials is reduced to a minimum. This can, of course, be very expensive, if it is conceived in terms of environmental control systems, significant building modifications, and the like. It can be done very cheaply, however, by simple housekeeping measures which are an integral part of the administration of a well-run library. Junior staff are the key to success. It is they who handle books and deal with users. They can act both as the detectors of the first signs of damage or decay, and as the exemplars in the handling and care of materials.

Good housekeeping begins with the shelves. Ideally, these should be of metal, not wood, since metal is not susceptible to the biological hazards which can beset any organic substance. Metal is easier to keep clean, and less likely to be broken or damaged. The proper care of books on the shelves is the starting-point of a preservation programme. This means, among other things, regular and careful dusting using soft dusters and no chemical cleaning medium. Even in heavily used reference collections, most books spend most of their lives on the shelves. Junior staff have to be taught to keep the shelves tidy, and in particular to ensure that they are always tidy at the beginning of the day. This has the psychological effect on users of encouraging them to try to maintain that level of tidiness, whereas untidy shelves can only become worse as time goes on.

A few simple rules also need to be applied by the professional staff in determining where and how books shall be stored. Outsize books should be shelved upright in a separate sequence, not foredge down in normally spaced shelves. Very large volumes, such as atlases or bound volumes of newspapers, should be shelved flat, even in open-access areas. Special shelving, or other storage systems, is needed for maps and audio-visual materials. Current parts of periodicals may need protective covers as a temporary measure before they go for boxing or binding. Pamphlets, again in a special sequence, are better stored in boxes than directly on the shelves. These are all simple matters of good practice, and are not beyond the realistic aspirations and capability of any library.

Staff and users alike should be exhorted to look after books. Staff should be encouraged not to overload trolleys, not to carry too many books, not to pile books too high on desks and tables or on or behind counters. Trolleys are needed for books returned to the circulation desk before they go for sorting and shelving. The trolleys should also be kept tidy, and, when they are moved, moved carefully. In all of these cases, exhortation is probably more effective than instruction, but it is also important that the professional staff make clear to juniors the extent and the limits of their authority in dealing with any recalcitrant users, and are then prepared to support them.

Staff in general need to be made aware that preservation is an aspect of collection management; otherwise some of this may seem a little trivial or pedantic. In particular, circulation staff should be empowered, and indeed required, to set aside books which are returned from loan in need of repair. This is not for the purpose of punishing a particular user who may or may not have been responsible for the damage. It is rather because a minor and cheap repair now may save the time and expense of a major repair later. A culture in which prevention is better than cure is created by example, and it is the responsibility of all professional staff to assist in its creation. In older buildings, all staff need to be alert for the first signs of serious biological events such as fungal growths, moulds and damp patches. A proper reporting system will be needed to ensure that any such suspicions reach the preservation manager, or other responsible professional, immediately.

Building design, the internal layout of the building, and furnishings are also critical elements in preservation. In research libraries, or in rare book rooms, it is essential that readers' tables are sufficiently generous in size to allow books to be used properly without piling them one on top of another. Where particularly valuable or fragile books and manuscripts are being used, table-top lecterns are essential; plastic forceps to hold the page open without exerting too much pressure on it are a useful additional precaution.

Some regulations are also necessary to ensure effective preservation. Apart from obvious rules about the use and misuse of books, it is normal to forbid the use of flat-platen photocopying machines with older books or manuscripts. Books in special collections are not normally available for circulation and are rarely loaned to other libraries, unless for exhibition under carefully regulated conditions. Although many of these considerations and regulations apply principally to older and more valuable materials, the general philosophy of concern and care which they imply can usefully be transferred to the general maintenance of the library's stock.

None of this will happen by itself. A library which wishes to create a preservation-conscious culture needs a senior member of staff responsible for it. In many, and perhaps most, libraries this is not a full-time job, and is perhaps most logically associated either with the post-holder responsible for collection management and development, or with the professional librarian with overall responsibility for the running of the building. The essential function of the preservation manager is that he or she has a general oversight of all the matters which we have been discussing, and is, therefore, in a position to have a policy-level view of the library's preservation situation. He or she is the determiner of the policies and priorities which will in turn allow logical and consistent decisions to be made in individual cases. The preservation manager also has some specific responsibilities. One, of great importance, is the compilation of the disaster preparedness plan. In some large academic and research libraries, and in most major record offices and archives, the post of preservation manager, under whatever title, is now a full-time senior position. Indeed, those libraries which have made most progress towards defining and solving their preservation problems have been those which have been prepared to invest in professional as well as technical personnel, so that long-term policies can be evolved and their implementation properly monitored.

The senior binders are among the most important advisers to the preservation manager, especially where the repair of older material is concerned. The final decisions are, of course, taken by the librarian, but it is important to recognize that the binder has his or her own expertise, and it should be exploited to the full. In particular, an experienced binder has a wide-ranging knowledge of materials and techniques which few if any professional librarians can equal. A binder is an implementer rather than an originator of policy, but typically has a fairly free hand within the broad outlines of institutional policies.

The senior binder also has to take on a managerial and administrative role in his or her own right, being in day-to-day charge of the bindery, and reporting to the preservation manager. This may be a fairly substantial task, although it should not be allowed to divert the binder too much from the regular work of the bindery. In a typical library bindery, operating on a modest scale, there will be one or two fully trained binders, and perhaps an apprentice. One of these people, usually the senior, may reserve for personal attention the exceptionally skilled tasks of finishing and decorating, especially in leather. Collating and sewing, regarded as less skilled and more functional work, are also usually separated off.[30]

The preservation manager also needs clerical support for the maintenance of records of work sent to the bindery and to outside companies, and for the general administration of the department. Administrative support becomes even more important if the manager is also responsible for a conservation laboratory, with one or two paper repairers and perhaps other scientists and technicians, or a photographic studio with camera operators, film processors and clerical assistance. The preservation brief, conceived in its broadest terms, covers so many aspects of the library's activities that it inevitably comes to occupy a major place among staff commitments.

Training for preservation

Preservation, as it is now generally understood and as it has been presented here, is a comparatively new element in librarianship, although it derives from many much older areas of activity and draws on long-established expertise. The present generation of preservation managers have generally come from one of two sources, although there are a few crucial exceptions. They were either conservators and bookbinders, or rare book librarians. It is clear that neither gives the ideal background or training for preservation as it is now practised. Until very recently, however, the library and information science schools have either neglected preservation altogether or have, like some libraries, marginalized it into such fields as rare book librarianship or archive studies. There is some evidence of improvement in this, and in the United Kingdom there has certainly been a growing awareness of the importance of the subject among educators since the low point recorded in the early 1980s.[31] By contrast, preservation has always been central to archives education; it is now recognized as having a managerial as well as a technical dimension.[32] Curriculum recommendations for both archives and librarianship students have recently been published, and will, it is hoped, influence developments in the next few years.[33]

It is essential that professional librarians are aware of preservation as a management issue in their institutions, but we have to recognize that no work can actually be carried out unless the relevant skills are available. We have already discussed the relative merits of in-house and external binderies, and referred to the salary differentials which often seem to exist between the two. In either case, however, trained personnel are essential. There is undoubtedly a skill shortage, especially in craft binding techniques, although it is said that the position is not as bad in the United Kingdom as it is in the United States.[34] On the other hand, even comparatively routine library work requires a craft binder, since a person who served an apprenticeship with the mechanized and increasingly automated techniques of case-binding will not have the necessary skills.[35] There has been a serious decrease in availability of these skills, and a decline in the attraction of binding as a career for a school-leaver.

The situation with regard to the training of binders, technicians and other benchworkers is somewhat confused. In the early 1980s, there were about 20 courses in Britain which appeared to be giving training in binding skills which were relevant to library and archive conservation,[36] but in the absence of any central validating body it is difficult to know what standards these courses attain. The Society of Archivists has responded to the needs of record offices by devising its own training schemes which have achieved a deservedly high reputation.[37] The need for paper repairers (the most important technical skill so far as archivists are concerned) is probably being met, but there is unquestionably a real problem in finding good craft binders. It has been argued that librarians should follow the example of the archivists, and provide their own training courses,[38] but it might reasonably be doubted whether there is really a demand on that scale, or funding to meet it if there is. The issue is further confused by the determination of some of the self-styled 'conservation binders' to draw a distinction between themselves and other craftsmen and to proclaim their own unique ability to use traditional craft methods.[39] There is no easy solution to the problem. Bookbinding is not a prestigious occupation, and it is not well paid. Commercial binderies will continue to be the main source of newly trained personnel, and it is perhaps inevitable that those companies will come to be even more dominant in library binding in Britain than they already are.

Conclusion
The management of a successful preservation programme is a joint venture between the librarian or archivist and the technician. But a great deal can be achieved without ever going near a bench or a studio. A properly managed library is one in which the information resource is properly protected, not so that it becomes a museum, but so that it can be used.

References
1 For a summary account of this, see Parry, D., *Newsplan. Report of the Newsplan Project in the northern region, October 1987 – September 1988*, London, The British Library, 1989, 2 – 5.

2 Wilson, A., *Library policy for preservation and conservation in the European Community. Principles, practices and the contribution of the new technology*, Munich, New York, London, Paris, K. G. Saur (CEC Publication EUR 11563), 1988, 30.

3 British Standards Institution, *Specification for 35 mm microcopying of newspapers for archival purposes*, London, British Standards Institution (BS 5847:1980), 1980. See also Library of Congress, *Specifications for the microfilming of newspapers in the Library of Congress*, Silver Spring, Md., Association for Information and Image Management, 1982.

4 See Parry, *Newsplan*, 56 – 9, 335 – 8.

5 Parry, *Newsplan*, 60 – 1. For a detailed American study, conducted in 1984, see McClung, P. A., 'Costs associated with preservation microfilming', 363 – 74.

6 Gordon, R., *Newsplan. Report of the Newsplan Project in the East Midlands, April 1987 – July 1988*, London, The British Library, 1989, 302 – 3.

7 Parry, *Newsplan*, 80 – 1.

8 Bailey, M. J., 'This works for us. Selecting titles for binding', *Special libraries*, **64**, 1973, 571 – 3.

9 See also Peacock, P. G., 'The selection of periodicals for binding', *Aslib proceedings*, **33**, 1981, 257 – 9.

10 Turner, J. 'Binding arbitration. A comparison of the durability of various hardback and paperback bindings', *Library Association record*, **88**, 1986, 233 – 5.

11 For a general study of some of these issues, see Streit, 'Transfer of materials', 33 – 46.

12 The point is made by Mowat, I. R. M., 'A policy proposal for the

conservation and control of bookstock in academic libraries', *Journal of librarianship*, **14**, 1982, 276.

13 Roberts, M., 'The role of the librarian in the binding process', *Special libraries*, **62**, 1971, 413 – 20.

14 Bansa, H., 'The awareness of conservation. Reasons for reorientation in library training', *Restaurator*, **7**, 1986, 36 – 47.

15 Turner, J. R., 'Teaching conservation', *Education for information*, **6**, 1988, 145 – 51.

16 Ratcliffe, *Preservation policies*, 17 – 18.

17 Banks, R. E. R., 'The commercial option: balancing needs and resources', in Palmer, *Preserving the word*, 77 – 89.

18 For a conservator's perspective, see Clarkson, C., 'Conservation priorities: a library conservator's view', in Petherbridge, G. (ed.), *Conservation of library and archive materials and the graphic arts*, London, Butterworth, 1987, 235 – 6.

19 Baynes-Cope, A. D., *Caring for books and documents*, 2nd ed., London, The British Library, 1989.

20 Conway, P. 'Archival preservation: definitions for improving education and training', *Restaurator*, **10**, 1989, 47 – 60.

21 Clements, D. W. G., 'Preservation microfilming and substitution policy in The British Library', *Microform review*, **17**, 1988, 17 – 22.

22 Wilson, *Library policy for preservation*, 20.

23 McClung, 'Costs associated with preservation microfilming', 363 – 74.

24. Enright, Hellinga and Leigh, *Selection for survival*, 36.

25 For descriptions of these and other practices, see Fitzgerald, 'Books and bindings', 73 – 7; and Langwell, W. H., *The conservation of books and documents*, London, Pitman, 1957, 91 – 103.

26 This figure is based on the author's recent experience in dealing with commercial binderies in the United Kingdom, while administering a British Library Wolfson Foundation grant to preserve the parish libraries of St Mary's Loughborough, and St Helen's, Ashby-de-la-Zouch.

27 For a useful summary of the options, see Rebsamen, W., 'Binding', *Library trends*, **30**, 1981 – 2, 225 – 39.

28 Henderson, C., 'Curator or conservator: who decides on what treatment', *Rare book and manuscript librarianship*, **2**, 1987, 103 – 7.

29 On this, see Mikovic, M., 'The binding of periodicals: basic concepts and procedures', *Serials librarian*, **11**, 1986, 93 – 118.

30 On bindery organization, see Clough, *Bookbinding for librarians*, 95 – 105.

31 For which see Ratcliffe, *Preservation policies*, 25 – 30. See also Hookway, Sir Harry, Dureau, J.-M., Ratcliffe, F. W., Clements, D. W. G., Forde, H. and Havard-Williams, P., 'Education for conservation', *Journal of librarianship*, **17**, 1985, 73 – 105; and Feather and Lusher, 'Education for conservation', 129 – 38.

32 Forde, H., 'Education and archive conservation', in National Preservation Office *Conservation in crisis*, (National Preservation Office Seminar Papers, 1), London, The British Library, 1987, 23 – 7.

33 Cook, M., *Guidelines for curriculum development in records management and the administration of modern archives: a RAMP study*, Paris, Unesco (PGI-82/WS/16), 1982, 14, 41 – 2; and Feather, J., *Guidelines on the teaching of preservation to librarians, archivists and documentalists*, The Hague, IFLA, forthcoming.

34 Stam, D. H., *National preservation planning in the United Kingdom: an American perspective*, London, The British Library (Research and Development Department Report, 5759), 1983, 3.

35 The present author has dealt with this at greater length in 'Manpower requirements in preservation', to be published in Mowat, I. R. M. (ed.), *Preservation administration*, Aldershot, Gower, forthcoming.

36 Bloomfield, B. C., 'Education and training for conservation work in the UK', in Ratcliffe, *Preservation policies*, 105 – 13.

37 Thomas, D., 'Training conservation technicians: an archivist's view', in Ratcliffe, *Preservation policies*, 125 – 6.

38 Ratcliffe, F. W., 'Education in preservation for librarians and conservators', in Palmer, *Preserving the word*, 104.

39 Most forcefully, at least in print, by Pickwoad, N., 'Conservation binding', in Ratcliffe, *Preservation policies*, 119 – 24.

7 *The professional context*

The design and implementation of preservation policy does not take place only at institutional level. It is sustained by regional, national and international policies and services. These reflect, in turn, the growing professional commitment which is found in the activities of national libraries, professional associations, governments and international organizations. This professional context has provided the essential background against which local developments have taken place over the last decade of intensified activity. It has significantly assisted those librarians who have been concerned with preservation in demonstrating to colleagues and paymasters alike the seriousness with which the profession as a whole has approached the issue.

As we have seen, the current concern with preservation really developed out of two immediate causes, one general and the other specific. The general cause was the growing awareness, in the 1960s, of the rapid deterioration of embrittled books and documents, especially in American libraries. The specific event was the Florence flood of 1966, which forced librarians to recognize the need to sustain the traditional skills of book restoration and repair. Of course, some librarians and most archivists had never lost their interest in preservation, although it was perhaps seen largely as a matter for those principally concerned with older materials in research libraries. It was rarely if ever linked to wider questions of collection management or to other and even broader professional concerns about access to information and information media. The purpose of this final chapter is to trace that process of change, not as a simple historical investigation, but rather to show the broad context within which preservation and collection management are properly placed.

Both the recognition of the embrittlement problem and the Florence flood had the incidental effect of forcing librarians to think about the co-operative and international aspects of preservation. The various

97

techniques of deacidification, for example, which so far offer the only means of preserving embrittled documents and books in their original format, were all developed with funding from national institutions, or from private-sector sponsors, with a view to providing central facilities which would be available to many different libraries and archives. The Library of Congress, one of the pioneers of deacidification, has consistently proclaimed its commitment to co-operation in preservation at both the national and the international level. It sees its optical disc experiments,[1] as well as its deacidification work, as being part of this contribution to solving the global preservation problem, and it has strongly supported international efforts to put preservation on the professional agenda.[2]

Co-operative efforts towards preservation, and in particular large-scale co-operative microfilming programmes, were one of the characteristic developments of the second half of the 1980s. They were widely commended in theory,[3] and although there were inevitable problems in implementing some individual projects,[4] there were also some notable successes.[5] The cost and scale of major surrogate creation programmes, like that of the development of new preservation technologies, was so large that only groups of institutions, with major financial backers, could undertake it. Indeed, the extent of the preservation problem, and the cost of the solutions to it, would have forced libraries to co-operate, even if they had not been willing to do so. Above all, however, co-operative information preservation came to be understood as the key to access and use, the twin lodestones of modern librarianship.[6] Co-operative collection development projects, with their wide implications for resource sharing and library funding arrangements, were also seen to have an important dimension, further propelling the issue to the forefront of professional concern.[7]

If the current interest in preservation as a tool of information management can be argued to have begun in the United States, there is no doubt that it has been enthusiastically received elsewhere in the world. It is perhaps helpful to begin by tracing recent developments and initiatives in the United Kingdom to illustrate the increasing pervasiveness of the issue and the general directions of development which are being evolved.

Throughout the 1970s, leading librarians in Britain, many of whom were in frequent and close contact with their opposite numbers in the United States, became increasingly aware of the preservation problem. As we have seen, it was made a major priority in the Reference Division of the newly created British Library. At the same time, other major institutions, such as the Bodleian Library, Oxford, reoriented their traditional binding and repair activities towards a more co-ordinated conservation programme.[8] All libraries which were concerned for the permanent retention of the greater part of their stocks began to recognize the need for active intervention to facilitate this, and to initiate appropriate programmes.[9]

The British Library was consistently the leader in this field of professional endeavour. As well as taking steps towards attacking its own preservation problems, it also helped to facilitate the development of national policies. In 1980, the Library's Research and Development Department commissioned Dr F. W. Ratcliffe, Librarian of Cambridge University, to conduct an investigation of preservation policies and practices in the United Kingdom.[10] It should be emphasized that this was quite unlike the preservation surveys which were by that time a fairly common feature of the library scene in the United States. Ratcliffe was principally concerned to gather information about facilities, personnel, training and attitudes rather than about books and documents. Indeed, a simultaneous investigation by David H. Stam, at that time Director of the Research Collections at New York Public Library, whose work was also funded by BLRDD, showed how different were British and American preservation problems and professional perceptions.[11]

The Ratcliffe and Stam reports provided the essential framework upon which national policies could be built. Although their approaches were in some ways quite different, they agreed in many of their conclusions. Both emphasized the need for the raising of professional and public awareness about the preservation issue. Both advocated greater national and international co-operation. Both pointed out the necessity of education and training for both professional and technical staff.[12] Many of these ideas bore fruit, and, in particular, the concept of awareness raising became central to the British response to the preservation crisis. The middle 1980s were difficult times for public-sector institutions in Britain. Large-scale new initiatives could only be funded either by diverting diminishing resources from existing activities, or by raising money in the private sector or from charitable foundations. All of these methods came to be used in due course, but the first step was clearly the need to establish a proper perception of the importance of preservation. The publication of the Ratcliffe Report was in itself a significant move in that direction.

Even more important was the almost immediate adoption of one of Ratcliffe's key recommendations, the establishment of what he called a 'national advisory and research centre'.[13] This idea was realized in late 1984, within months of the publication of the Ratcliffe Report, by the establishment within the British Library of the National Preservation Office (NPO), which has come to play a central strategic role in library preservation in the United Kingdom. Its role is partly advisory, both in helping smaller libraries with their preservation problems and in giving policy advice at every level, and partly educational, supporting conferences and promotional activities of various kinds.[14] The National Preservation Advisory Committee (NPAC), which works to it, links NPO into the profession at large by a complex structure of representation from all sectors of librarianship, as well as from the archives field and from professional associations and organizations. NPAC's subsidiary panels, one of conservators and one of educators, have carried its work forward into two areas of particular concern, skill training and professional education.

The need to raise awareness among British librarians and funding bodies has been reflected in many NPO activities. An annual series of seminars, beginning in 1986,[15] has brought together 40 or 50 of the most committed librarians, archivists and educators on a regular basis. It has also provided the papers for a series of useful publications in a field in which up-to-date British literature was in short supply. With financial support either from the Preservation Service or from the Research and Development Department, the NPO has also been involved in projects on disaster preparedness planning,[16] and curriculum development.[17] It is associated with the publication of the British Library's *Library conservation news*, an invaluable source of information about the preservation field in the United Kingdom. Private-sector support has provided the funding for annual prizes for the best conservation project in a British library, and, from 1990, a prize for the best essay on a preservation theme by a student in a British library school.[18] The NPO is now moving into a new phase of activity in which it is publishing bibliographies,[19] making data available through the British Library's on-line information networks, and acting as a clearing house for information on techniques, materials, suppliers and personnel.

Neither the National Preservation Office, nor indeed the British Library itself, has a directive role, but both can exert great influence. The increased awareness of preservation needs has led to greater emphasis on preservation in professional practice. In turn, this has also made it possible to raise funding for specific projects. The Wolfson Foundation, for example, has donated substantial funds, administered by the British Library, for preservation work in smaller collections throughout the country.[20] More recently, the Mellon Foundation has given US\$3 million for preservation microfilming, and associated activities in the legal deposit libraries of the United Kingdom and at Trinity College, Dublin.[21] Even the British government has been moved to generosity. The Minister for the Arts announced in 1989 the establishment of a special fund for the conservation and repair of manuscripts and archives.[22]

This account of British Library and NPO activities in preservation – all, it should be remembered, in addition to the Library's very considerable in-house programmes – is by no means exhaustive, for important new initiatives are coming on-stream all the time. However, it is enough to give some idea of the range and depth of the British Library's involvement, and its interpretation of its national leadership role. Most major libraries in Britain now take preservation very seriously indeed; even in the public libraries there is both enthusiasm and commitment in some cases. Of course, there are still serious gaps in provision. Funding is needed for the second and more important phase of *Newsplan*, the filming of the newspapers themselves. The first phase alone, however, which is completing the bibliographic record of UK newspapers, and providing records of holdings, is in itself an invaluable scholarly tool.[23] There are many smaller libraries with historically and bibliographically significant holdings which are still in need of assessment and treatment. There is still a serious shortage of skilled craftsmen. There is still a high degree of ignorance among some professional librarians. Above all, the calls on diminishing library budgets are becoming larger and more complex. Yet there has been some change; and from the position which Ratcliffe and Stam so graphically described less than a decade ago, change could only be for the better.[24]

The development of national policies inevitably mirrors both national cultural preoccupations and national political structures. Thus, the British Library must lead by example and exhortation, and in recent years has had to seek external funding for many activities as well as looking to generate income from some of its operations. In some countries, however, the national library or its sponsoring ministry can enforce policy on the nation's library system as a whole. Governments even pay for implementation. In France, for example, the Bibliothèque nationale itself has to some extent taken the lead by establishing its own

101

Centre de conservation at the Château de Sablé, but the ministries responsible for libraries have also played key roles. As a consequence, France is considered by one knowledgable and astute commentator to have the most systematic library preservation programme among all the member states of the European Community.[25] The Bibliothèque nationale itself established its own *Plan de sauvegarde* in 1979. This followed on from the report of the Caillet Commission, which had, in effect, conducted a massive preservation survey of the library's holdings. The government provided an annual budget of no less than FF10 million from 1980 onwards to implement the plan. This included the establishment of new studios and workshops, the initiation of huge microfilming and repair programmes, and support for research and development work in deacidification. In France, as elsewhere, the scale of need far outstretches the scale of provision, and even the exceptional generosity of the French government is inadequate to meet the massive needs of the Bibliothèque nationale.[26]

Nationally, French policies evolved from the report of the Desgraves Commission in 1982, substantially adopted in 1984.[27] This report, sponsored by the Direction du livre et de la lecture in the Ministry of Culture, was particularly concerned with the widespread preservation problems to be found in France's historic public libraries, the *bibliothèques municipales*. Unlike most of their British and American counterparts, the French public libraries have large and important holdings of old and rare material, much of it derived from the pre-revolutionary private and ecclesiastical libraries which formed their foundation collections at the turn of the eighteenth and nineteenth centuries, when they were confiscated from their former owners. The Desgraves report recommended a wide range of measures, including the establishment of regional centres for conservation and microfilming work; better provision for the exploitation of collections through the creation and dissemination of guides, inventories and catalogues; and programmes of education and training for professional and technical staff and of awareness raising for users and the general public.[28] Some of this has been effected. Regional centres exist, a union catalogue of microfilmed newspapers was published in 1988, and there has been a good deal of educational activity.[29]

Just as French experience reflects the strong centrifugal tendencies of the French state (at least until the middle 1980s), so the recent history of preservation in Germany reflects the strength of that country's regional structures. There is no single national library, but there are very important regional research libraries. Reflecting, no doubt, the important historical role of the scholar-librarian in German culture, a scholar rather than a librarian was commissioned to undertake the national preservation survey, although it should be added that he is a distinguished student of the history of books and libraries. Not surprisingly, he produced a report which reflected both his own humanistic interests and his long-standing knowledge of the British Library and of British and American traditions of bibliographical scholarship.[30] In the follow-up to the Fabian Report, a working group of the Deutsche Forschungsgemeinschaft, which co-ordinates inter-regional resource sharing among the libraries of Germany produced a number of specific recommendations. Most of these were concerned with access to materials and with union cataloguing rather than with preservation *per se*, although one recommendation did deal with the need for central conservation facilities for the treatment of important historical materials.[31]

Many other European countries, both east and west, have undertaken preservation surveys; some have subsequently initiated programmes to act on the results. There are many common problems, in terms of underfunding, neglect of collections, unsuitable buildings, and lack of conservation facilities and expertise, as well as failure on the part of officials, librarians and users to understand the urgency and seriousness of the problem.[32]

Within the European Community, there have been the beginnings of library co-operation between the member states at Community level. This has been at least as true in preservation as in other spheres of library and information activity. Alexander Wilson's survey of 1986 – 7 has already been cited several times,[33] and is an invaluable account of the situation in the 12 states at a time when the major EC library initiatives were in the planning stage. Wilson was particularly concerned with information technology applications in preservation, but he interpreted his brief widely enough to be able to include scientific developments such as deacidification research and the use of photographic and digitized surrogate media for information preservation. Little truly inter-state collaboration was revealed, but he suggested a number of areas in which it might be developed. These included support for inter-state catalogues, the funding of relevant research and development and the encourage-ment of educational initiatives.[34]

One specific recommendation, which has been followed through to some extent, was that which suggested the promotion of co-operative microfilming projects. In 1988 – 9, Directorate-General XIII-B of the Commission of the Community, which is responsible for the draft Action Plan for Libraries, commissioned a feasibility study for a European Register of Microform Masters, a project which had also been supported by LIBER, the Ligue Internationale des Bibliothèques Européennes de Recherche. The consultants' report was confidential, but it is known to have suggested both a rationale and a methodology for developing such a register in machine-readable form.[35] In fact, the British Library and the Bibliothèque nationale are already exchanging machine-readable bibliographic records of archival master negatives, and the U K and Irish libraries in receipt of Mellon funding for preservation microfilming will be adding their records into the same file in due course. This provides the basis for a European equivalent of the long-established *National register of microform masters* published by the Library of Congress. It will help to eliminate expensive duplication of effort, and at the same time facilitate access to rare, valuable and often fragile materials.

When we go beyond Europe, we find that within the wider international library community, IFLA has played a critical role in promoting the preservation issue. A Core Programme in Preservation and Conservation (PAC) was established in 1984,[36] and has been active ever since. PAC is based at the Library of Congress, but it has also established a number of regional centres around the world. The purpose of these centres is to act as referral agencies, information disseminators and trainers for both professionals and technicians from the countries of their respective regions. At present there are PAC centres established at Leipzig in Germany (for eastern Europe),[37] in the Bibliothèque nationale's Sablé facility (for western Europe and francophone Africa),[38] at Caracas in Venezuela (for Latin America),[39] and most recently, at the National Diet Library in Tokyo (for east Asia) and the National Library of Australia (for Australasia).

Education, training and awareness raising lie at the heart of PAC's mission. The formal launch of the programme took place at a meeting of the Conference of Directors of National Libraries held in Vienna in 1986. This meeting, jointly sponsored by IFLA and Unesco, took as one of its themes the need for education and training for preservation.[40] Training seminars for librarians and conservators from eastern Europe have been held at Leipzig (in 1986), and for those from francophone Africa at Sablé (in 1989); a similar seminar for anglophone African library and archive directors was held in London and at

Loughborough in the United Kingdom in 1990.

This does not complete the list of PAC's activities, many of which have been undertaken in collaboration with IFLA's Section on Conservation. Perhaps the most important to reach fruition so far was the compilation of guidelines on conservation edited by David Clements and Jeanne-Marie Dureau,[41] a document intended to help librarians to begin their preservation planning and policy-making. Projects in progress include the Conservation Information Data base (CID), being compiled by various national contributors and co-ordinated by PAC in Washington. CID is designed to contain bibliographic references (with abstracts) to publications on preservation and related matters issued since 1960 throughout the world.

Finally, Unesco has also been active in the field of library preservation in several respects. In a sense, this brings us full circle, for it was Unesco which co-ordinated the rescue efforts at Florence which some now see as the begining of the revival of interest in conservation and preservation. Increasingly, however, preservation has come to be seen in Unesco, as elsewhere, as an aspect of information service provision rather than being solely a matter of cultural heritage. Many of Unesco's most important recent initiatives in the library preservation field have been under the auspices of PGI, the Programme Générale d'Information. In particular, the Records and Archives Management Programme (RAMP) has assumed a far wider role than its title might suggest. A considerable number of studies have been commissioned and published, including documents on environmental conditions in library and archives buildings, disaster preparedness planning and pest management. Some of these have already been cited in previous chapters, because they are often the most current and the most authoritative accounts of their respective subjects.[42] Other RAMP projects are in progress. These include a major study of the world's cultural patrimony (defined in this case, perhaps rather narrowly, as books, manuscripts and documents) being undertaken under the joint auspices of RAMP, IFLA and the International Council on Archives.[43]

International conferences, Unesco reports and European Commission plans can sometimes seem a little remote from the work of the ordinary librarian or archivist, struggling to keep a decaying collection in a condition in which it can be used, often in an inadequate building and almost always with insufficient funds. The perception is understandable, but it is false. A profession, which is, by definition, self-regulating, creates for itself the climate in which it conducts its activities. Within the broad scope of providing the service demanded by its clients, it largely determines its own agenda. In the last 20 years, and more markedly so during the 1980s, the library profession in many countries has apparently reached the conclusion, through its various representative bodies, that preservation is an area of significant and serious professional concern. The infrastructure of support which is offered by national, international and supranational bodies, and the policies which they can determine or influence, is the essential foundation upon which action is built. Most libraries in most countries are heavily dependent upon public funding, and public funding is voted by politicians who themselves, in democratic states, have to be sensitive to public opinion. Preservation is not, of course, a major public concern (although conservation in general is an increasingly prominent political issue throughout the industrialized world), but opinion-formers and professional leaders have succeeded in putting it on the official agenda.

A consensus is emerging which will carry us through the new decade and into a new century. There is a broad general agreement that preservation is important, not least because our central professional activity – to transfer information from source to user – will be frustrated if we lose the media which contain the information. Therefore we need to be able to determine whether to preserve information in its original format, or whether to reformat it and preserve the surrogate. We need to have the technologies which will permit the reformatting to take place, and then to preserve the surrogates themselves. We need to be able to repair, restore and preserve those damaged originals which we prefer not to sacrifice. In short, ten years of revitalized concern for the physical media of information have forced us to rethink the way in which we manage our information resources.

Preservation, access and use are interdependent, not contradictory. Preservation is properly seen as one aspect of collection management, the process by which library collections are assembled, augmented and organized for exploitation. It is concerned with all formats and all media. It is concerned with the old and the new. It is concerned with the past. But it is, above all, vitally concerned with the future.

References

1   Welsh, W. J., 'Experiments with optical disk technology at the Library of Congress', *IATUL proceedings*, **18**, 1986, 41 – 9.
2   Welsh, W. J., 'International cooperation in preservation of library

materials', *Collection management*, **9**, 1987, 119 – 31.

3 See, for example, Govan, 'Preservation and resource sharing', 20 – 4; Jolliffe, J., 'International cooperation in preservation', *Collection management*, **9**, 1987, 113 – 18; and Merrill-Oldham, J., 'Preservation comes of age. An action agenda for the '80s and beyond', *American libraries*, **116**, 1985, 771.

4 Gwinn, N. E., 'The rise and fall and rise of cooperative projects', *Library resources and technical services*, **29**, 1985, 80 – 6.

5 See, for example, Dupont, J. 'Cooperative microform publishing: the law library experience', *Microform review*, **12**, 1983, 234 – 8; and Markham, R., 'Religion converted to microformat', *Microform review*, **16**, 1987, 217 – 23.

6 Line, 'Interlending and conservation: friends or foes?', 7 – 11; and Wilson, A., 'For this and future generations: managing the conflict between conservation and use', *Library review*, **31**, 1982, 163 – 72.

7 Stam, D. H., 'Collaborative collection development'; for an update, see Battin, P., 'Cooperative preservation in the United States: progress and possibilities', *Alexandria*, **1**, 1989, 7 – 16.

8 Turner, M. L., 'Conservation in the Bodleian: a case study', in Ratcliffe, *Preservation policies*, 127 – 31.

9 See, for example, Price, R., 'Preserving the word: conservation in the Wellcome Institute Library', in National Preservation Office, *Conservation in crisis*, 49 – 55.

10 Published in 1984 as Ratcliffe, *Preservation policies*.

11 Issued in 1983 as Stam, *National preservation planning*.

12 There is a useful summary of their conclusions in Wilson, *Library policy for preservation*, 92 – 6.

13 Ratcliffe, *Preservation policies*, 36 – 8.

14 Clements, D. W. G., 'The National Preservation Office in the British Library', *IFLA journal*, **12**, 1986, 25 – 32.

15 The first was published in 1987 as *Conservation in crisis*.

16 Published as Tregarthen Jenkin, *Disaster planning*.

17 Published as Feather, J. and Lusher, A., *The teaching of conservation in LIS schools in Great Britain*, London, The British Library (Research Paper, 49), 1988.

18 National Preservation Office/Riley, Dunn and Wilson, *Keeping our words. The 1988 National Preservation Office competition*, London, The British Library, 1989.

19 For example, National Preservation Office, *Bibliography. Audiovisual materials on preservation*, London, The British Library, [1989].

20 'Awards for cataloguing, preservation and purchase', *The British Library Research and Development Department research bulletin*, **3**, Spring 1989, 5 – 7.

21 'US gift of $1.5m for microfilming at BL', *Library and information news*, February 1989, 18.

22 'Arts Minister launches National Manuscripts Conservation Trust, *Library conservation news*, **26**, January 1990, 3.

23 Johansson, E., 'National approaches to newspaper preservation: the United Kingdom', in Gibb, *Newspaper preservation and access*, vol. 2, 349 – 50; Gordon, *Newsplan*; Parry, *Newsplan*; and Wells, R., *Newsplan. Report of the pilot project in the South-West*, London, The British Library (Library and Information Report, 38), 1986.

24 For an authoritative survey, see Ratcliffe, F.W., 'Preservation: a decade of progress', *Library review*, **36**, 1987, 228 – 36.

25 Wilson, *Library policy for preservation*, 66.

26 Wilson, *Library policy for preservation*, 76 – 8.

27 France, Ministère de la culture, *Le patrimoine des bibliothèques*, Paris, Ministère de la culture, 1982.

28 Wilson, *Library policy for preservation*, 68 – 75.

29 Clements, D. W. G. and Arnoult, J.-M., 'Preservation planning in Europe', *IFLA journal*, **14**, 1988, 356.

30 Fabian, B., *Buch, Bibliothek und Geisteswissenschaftliche Forschung*, Göttingen, Vandenhoek und Ruprecht, 1983.

31 Kaltwasser, F. G., 'Probleme der Literaturversorung in den Geisteswissenschaften', *ZIBB*, **33**, 1986, 92 – 9.

32 For a survey, see Clements and Arnoult, 'Preservation planning in Europe', *passim*; and also the papers presented at an IFLA/PAC seminar held in Leipzig in May 1986, available in typescript from the PAC Regional Centre at Sablé, France. The papers on Austria, by Magda Strebl, on Czechoslovakia by M. Velinsky, and on the USSR by S. P. Dvoriashina are particularly illuminating, although we have to assume that the situation may have changed in some eastern European countries in recent months.

33 Published as Wilson, *Library policy for preservation*.

34 Wilson, *Library policy for preservation*, 138 – 40.

35 Feather, J., 'Towards a European Register of Microform Masters (EROMM)', *Outlook on research libraries*, **11**, 1989, 4 – 5.

36 Smith, M. A., 'The IFLA Core Program in Preservation and Conservation (PAC)', *IFLA journal*, **12**, 1986, 305 – 6.

37 Wächter, W., 'Mechanising restoration work – the Deutsche Bucherei, Leipzig, and its role as a regional centre for IFLA', *IFLA journal*, **12**, 1986, 307 – 9.

38 Arnoult, J.-M., 'Le Centre de conservation de la Bibliothèque nationale au Château de Sablé', *IFLA journal*, **12**, 1986, 309 – 10.

39 Blanco, L., 'PAC Regional Center: Caracas', *International preservation news*, **3**, 1988, 1 – 4.

40 Published as Smith, *Preservation of library materials.*
41 Published as Clements, D.W.G. and Dureau, J.-M., *Principles for the preservation and conservation of library materials*, The Hague, IFLA, 1986.
42 For a list, see Conseil internationale des archives, *Publications*, Paris, CIA/ICA, 1988, 24 – 30.
43 For a fuller account of this and other international aspects of preservation, see Feather, J., 'National and international policies for preservation', *International library review*, forthcoming.

Bibliography

American National Standards Institute, *American National Standard for Information Science – Permanence of paper for printed library materials*, New York, ANSI (ANSI Z39.48-1984), 1984.

Arnoult, J.-M., 'Le Centre de conservation de la Bibliothèque nationale au Château de Sablé', *IFLA journal*, **12**, 1986, 309 – 10.

Arnoult, J.-M., 'Mass deacidification at the Bibliothèque nationale', in Smith, M. A. (ed.), *Preservation of library materials* (Conference held at the National Library of Austria, Vienna, 7 – 19 April 1986, sponsored by the Conference of Directors of National Libraries in co-operation with IFLA and Unesco), 2 vols, Munich, London, New York, Paris, K. G. Saur (IFLA Publications, 40, 41), 1987, vol. 2, 129 – 33.

Bailey, M. J., 'This works for us. Selecting titles for binding', *Special libraries*, **64**, 1973, 571 – 73.

Banks, R. E. R., 'The commercial option: balancing needs and resources', in Palmer, R. E. (ed.), *Preserving the word* (Library Association Conference Proceedings, Harrogate, 1986), London, The Library Association, 1987, 77 – 89.

Bansa, H., 'The awareness of conservation. Reasons for reorientation in library training', *Restaurator*, **7**, 1986, 36 – 47.

Battin, P., 'Cooperative preservation in the United States: progress and possibilities', *Alexandria*, **1**, 1989, 7 – 16.

Battin, P., 'Preservation at the Columbia University libraries', in Merrill-Oldham, J. and Smith, M. (eds.), *The Library Preservation program. Models, priorities, possibilities*, Chicago, Ill., American Library Association, 1985, 34 – 40.

Baynes – Cope, A. D., *Caring for books and documents*, 2nd ed., London, The British Library, 1989.

Beard, J. C., 'Preservation problems in public libraries', in Palmer, R. E. (ed.), *Preserving the word* (Library Association Conference Proceedings, Harrogate, 1986), London, The Library Association, 1987, 46 – 50.

Blanco, L., 'PAC Regional Center: Caracas', *International preservation news*, **3**, 1988, 1 – 4.

Bloomfield, B. C., 'Education and training for conservation work in the U. K.', in Ratcliffe, F. W., *Preservation policies and conservation in British libraries: Report of the Cambridge University Library Conservation Project*, London, The British Library (Library and Information Research Report, 25), 1984, 105 – 13.

Bohem, H., *Disaster prevention and disaster preparedness*, Berkeley, Calif., University of California Press, 1978.

Bond, R., DeCarlo, M., Henes, E. and Snyder, E., 'Preservation study at the Syracuse University Libraries', *College and research libraries*, **48**, 1987, 132 – 47.

Bourke, T. A., 'The New York Public Library Register of Microform Masters', *Microform review*, **13**, 1984 – 5, 17 – 21.

British Leather Manufacturers' Research Association, *The conservation of bookbinding leather*, London, The British Library, 1984.

The British Library, *Annual report 1974 – 75*, London, The British Library, 1975.

The British Library, *Annual report 1980–81*, London, The British Library, 1981.

The British Library, *Annual report 1983–84*, London, The British Library, 1984.

The British Library, *Annual report 1986–87*, London, The British Library, 1987.

The British Library, *Annual report 1988–89*, London, The British Library, 1989.

The British Library, *First annual report*, London, The British Library, 1974.

British Standards Institution, *Recommendations for the storage and exhibition of archival documents*, London, British Standards Institution (BS 5454:1977), 1977.

British Standards Institution, *Specification for 35 mm microcopying of newspapers for archival purposes*, London, British Standards Institution (BS 5847:1980), 1980.

Brown, L. H., 'Preservation in original format: the role of paper quality', in Smith, M. A. (ed.), *Preservation of library materials* (Conference held at the National Library of Austria, Vienna, 7 – 19 April 1986, sponsored by the Conference of Directors of National Libraries in co-operation with IFLA and Unesco), 2 vols, Munich, London, New York, Paris, K. G. Saur (IFLA Publications, 40, 41), 1987, vol. 1, 49 – 58.

Buchanan, S. A., *Disaster planning: preparedness and recovery for libraries and archives*, Paris, Unesco (PGI-88/WS/6), 1988.

Burton, J. O., 'Permanence studies of current commercial book papers', *Bureau of Standards journal of research*, **7**, 1931, 429 – 39.

Cannon, T., 'A review of the new technologies', in National Preservation Office, *Preservation and technology* (National Preservation Office Seminar Papers, 3), London, The British Library, 1989, 47 – 52.

Clarkson, C., 'Conservation priorities: a library conservator's view', in Petherbridge, G. (ed.), *Conservation of library and archive materials and the graphic arts*, London, Butterworth, 1987, 233 – 56.

Clarkson, L. A., 'Developments in tanning methods during the post-medieval period (1500 – 1850)', in East Midlands Industrial Archaeology Conference,

Leather manufacturing through the ages, Leicester, Leicester University Press, 1983.

Clements, D. W. G., 'The National Preservation Office in the British Library', *IFLA journal*, **12**, 1986, 25 – 32.

Clements, D. W. G., *Preservation and conservation of library documents: a Unesco/IFLA/ICA enquiry into the current state of the world's patrimony*, Paris, Unesco (PGI-87/WS/15), 1987

Clements, D. W. G., 'Preservation in original format: policies and options', in Smith, M. A. (ed.), *Preservation of library materials* (Conference held at the National Library of Austria, Vienna, 7 – 19 April 1986, sponsored by the Conference of Directors of National Libraries in co-operation with IFLA and Unesco), 2 vols, Munich, London, New York, Paris, K. G. Saur (IFLA Publications, 40, 41), 1987, vol. 1, 43 – 8.

Clements, D. W. G., 'Preservation microfilming and substitution policy in The British Library', *Microform review*, **17**, 1988, 17 – 22.

Clements, D. W. G. and Arnoult, J. – M., 'Preservation planning in Europe', *IFLA journal*, **14**, 1988, 354 – 60.

Clements, D. W. G. and Dureau, J. – M., *Principles for the preservation and conservation of library materials*, The Hague, IFLA, 1986.

Clough, E. A., *Bookbinding for librarians*, London, Association of Assistant Librarians, 1957.

Conseil internationale des archives, *Publications*, Paris, CIA/ICA, 1988.

Conway, P., 'Archival preservation: definitions for improving education and training', *Restaurator*, **10**, 1989, 47 – 60.

Cook, M., *Guidelines for curriculum development in records management and the administration of modern archives: a RAMP study*, Paris, Unesco (PGI-82/WS/16), 1982.

Cunha, G. M., *Methods to determine the preservation needs in libraries and archives: a RAMP study with guidelines*, Paris, Unesco (PGI-88/WS/160), 1988.

Cunha, G. M. and Cunha, D. G., *Libraries and archives conservation: 1980s and beyond*, Metuchen, N J, Scarecrow Press, 1983.

Cunha, G. M., Lowell, H. P. and Schnare, R. E., Jr, *Conservation survey manual*, New York, New York Library Association, 1982.

Dachs, K., 'Conservation: the curator's point of view', *Restaurator*, **6**, 1984, 118 – 26.

Diehl, E., *Bookbinding. Its background and technique*, 2 vols, New York, Rinehart, 1946.

Dupont, J., 'Cooperative microform publishing: the law library experience', *Microform review*, **12**, 1983, 234 – 8.

Enright, B., Hellinga, L. and Leigh, B., *Selection for survival. A review of acquisition and retention policies*, London, The British Library, 1989.

Fabian, B., *Buch, bibliothek und Geisteswissenschaftliche Forschung*, Göttingen, Vandenhoek und Ruprecht, 1983.

Feather, J., *Guidelines on the teaching of preservation to librarians, archivists and documentalists*, The Hague, IFLA, forthcoming.

Feather, J., 'Manpower requirements in preservation', in Mowat, I. R. M. (ed.), *Preservation administration*, Aldershot, Gower, forthcoming.

Feather, J., 'National and international policies for preservation', *International library review*, forthcoming.

Feather J., 'Towards a European Register of Microform Masters (EROMM)', *Outlook on research libraries*, **11**, 1989, 4 – 5.

Feather, J. and Lusher, A., 'Education for conservation in British library schools: current practices and future prospects', *Journal of librarianship*, **21**, 1989, 129 – 38.

Feather, J. and Lusher, A., *The teaching of conservation in LIS schools in Great Britain*, London, The British Library (Research Paper, 49), 1988.

Fitzgerald, A., 'Books and bindings', in Swartzburg, S. G. (ed.), *Conservation in the library. A handbook of use and care of traditional and nontraditional materials*, London, Aldwych Press, 1983, 55 – 78.

Forde, H., 'Education and archive conservation' in National Preservation Office, *Conservation in crisis* (National Preservation Office Seminar Papers, 1), London, The British Library, 1987, 23 – 7.

France, Ministère de la culture, *Le patrimoine des bibliothèques*, Paris, Ministère de la culture, 1982.

Gibb, I. (ed.), *Newspaper preservation and access* (Symposium held in London, 12 – 15 August 1987), 2 vols, Munich, New York, London, Paris, K. G. Saur (IFLA Publications, 45, 46), 1988.

Gordon, R., *Newsplan. Report of the Newsplan Project in the East Midlands, April 1987 – July 1988*, London, The British Library, 1989.

Govan, J. F., 'Preservation and resource sharing: conflicting or complementary?', *IFLA journal*, **12**, 1986, 20 – 4.

Gwinn, N. E. (ed.), *Preservation microfilming. A guide for librarians and archivists*, Chicago, Ill., London, American Library Association, 1987.

Gwinn, N. E., 'The rise and fall and rise of cooperative projects', *Library resources and technical services*, **29**, 1985, 80 – 6.

Gwinn, N. E. and Mosher, P. H., 'Coordinating collection development: the RLG Conspectus', *College and research libraries*, **44**, 1983, 128 – 40.

Harrison, H. P., 'Conservation and audio-visual materials', *Audio-visual librarian*, **13**, 1987, 154 – 62.

Heckmann, H., 'Storage and handling of audio and magnetic materials', in Smith, M. A. (ed.), *Preservation of library materials* (Conference held at the National Library of Austria, Vienna, 7 – 19 April 1986, sponsored by the Conference of Directors of National Libraries in co-operation with IFLA and Unesco), 2 vols, Munich, London, New York, Paris, K. G. Saur (IFLA Publications, 40, 41), 1987, vol. 2, 67 – 73.

Henderson, C., 'Curator or conservator: who decides on what treatment',

Rare book and manuscript librarianship, **2**, 1987, 103 – 7.

Hendley, T., *The archival storage potential of microfilm, magnetic media and optical data discs*, Hatfield, National Reprographic Centre for Documentation (BNB Research Fund Report, 10), 1983.

Hendricks, K. B., *The preservation and restoration of photographic materials in archives and libraries*, Paris, Unesco (PGI-84/WS/1), 1984.

Hendricks, K. B., 'Storage and handling of photographic materials', in Smith, M. A. (ed.), *Preservation of library materials* (Conference held at the National Library of Austria, Vienna, 7 – 19 April 1986, sponsored by the Conference of Directors of National Libraries in co-operation with IFLA and Unesco), 2 vols, Munich, London, New York, Paris, K. G. Saur (IFLA Publications, 40, 41), 1987, vol. 2, 55 – 66.

Hookway, Sir Harry, Dureau, J. – M., Ratcliffe, F. W., Clements, D. W. G., Ford, H. and Havard-Williams, P., 'Education for conservation', *Journal of librarianship*, **17**, 1985, 73 – 105.

Hunter, D., *Papermaking. The history and technique of an ancient craft*, 2nd ed., New York, Knopf, 1947.

Hutton, B. G., 'Preservation policy at the National Library of Scotland in Palmer, R. E. (ed.), *Preserving the word* (Library Association Conference Proceedings, Harrogate, 1986), London, The Library Association, 1987, 26 – 8.

Hutton, B. G., 'Preserving Scotland's heritage', *Library conservation news*, **19**, April 1988, 1 – 3.

Irvine, R. and Woodhead, G. S., 'On the presence in paper of residual chemicals used in its preparation', *Journal of the Society of the Chemical Industry*, **13**, 1894, 131 – 3.

Jarrell, T. D. (ed.), *Deterioration of book and record papers*, Washington, DC, Department of Agriculture, 1936.

Johansson, E., 'National approaches to newspaper preservation: the United Kingdom', in Gibb, I. P. (ed.), *Newspaper preservation and access* (Proceedings of a symposium held in London, 12 – 15 August 1987), 2 vols, Munich, New York, London, Paris, K. G. Saur, 1988, vol. 2, 349 – 50.

Johnson, R., 'Inferior paper', *Library journal*, **16**, 1891, 241 – 2.

Jolliffe, J., 'International cooperation in preservation', *Collection management*, **9**, 1987, 113 – 18.

Kalina, C. R., 'Acid-free paper for biomedical literature', *Scholarly publishing*, **19**, 1988, 217 – 20.

Kaltwasser, F. G., 'Probleme der Literaturversorung in den Geisteswissenschaften', *ZIBB*, **33**, 1986, 92 – 9.

Kovacs, B., 'Preservation of materials in science and technology libraries', *Science and technology libraries*, **7**, 1987, 3 – 13.

Langwell, W. H., *The conservation of books and documents*, London, Pitman, 1957.

114

Library Association, *The durability of paper*, London, The Library Association, 1930.

Library Association, National Preservation Office, and the Publishers' Association, *Permanent paper*, London, The Library Association, 1986.

Library of Congress, *Specifications for the microfilming of newspapers in the Library of Congress*, Silver Spring, Md., Association for Information and Image Management, 1982.

Library of Congress, Preservation Office, *A national preservation program. Proceedings of a planning conference*, Washington, DC, Library of Congress, 1980.

Line, M. B., 'Interlending and conservation: friends or foes?', *Interlending and document supply*, 16, 1988, 7-11.

Lynch, C. A. and Brownrigg, E. B., 'Conservation, preservation and digitization', *College and research libraries*, 47, 1986, 379-84.

McClung, P. A., 'Costs associated with preservation microfilming: results of the Research Libraries Group study', *Library resources and technical services*, 30, 1986, 363-74.

Markham, R., 'Religion converted to microformat', *Microform review*, 16, 1987, 217 – 23.

Meadows, A. J., 'The medium and the message', in National Preservation Office, *Preservation and technology* (National Preservation Office Seminar Papers, 3), London, The British Library, 1989, 1 – 9.

Merrill-Oldham, J., 'Preservation comes of age. An action agenda for the '80s and beyond', *American libraries*, 116, 1985, 770 – 2.

Merrill-Oldham, J. and Smith, M. (eds.), *The Library Preservation Program. Models, priorities, possibilities*, Chicago, Ill., American Library Association, 1985.

Middleton, B. C., *A history of English craft bookbinding technique*, 3rd ed., London, The Holland Press, 1988.

Mikovic, M., 'The binding of periodicals: basic concepts and procedures', *Serials librarian*, 11, 1986, 93 – 118.

Moon, B. E. and Loveday, A. J., 'Progress report on preservation in universities since the Ratcliffe Report', in National Preservation Office, *Preservation and technology* (National Preservation Office Seminar Papers, 3), London, The British Library, 1989, 11 – 17.

Morrow, C. C., *The preservation challenge. A guide to conserving library materials*, White Plains, NY, Knowledge Industry Publications, 1983.

Mowat, I. R. M., 'A policy proposal for the conservation and control of bookstock in academic libraries', *Journal of librarianship*, 14, 1982, 266 – 78.

Mowat, I. R. M., 'Preservation problems in academic libraries', in Palmer, R. E. (ed.), *Preserving the word* (Library Association Conference Proceedings, Harrogate, 1986), London, The Library Association, 1987, 37 – 45.

National Library of Scotland, *Planning manual for disaster control in Scottish libraries and record offices*, Edinburgh, National Library of Scotland, 1985.

National Preservation Office, *Bibliography. Audiovisual materials on preservation*, London, The British Library, [1989].

National Preservation Office, *Conservation in crisis* (National Preservation Office Seminar Papers, 1), London, The British Library, 1987.

National Preservation Office, *Preservation and technology* (National Preservation Office Seminar Papers, 3), London, The British Library, 1989.

National Preservation Office/Riley, Dunn and Wilson, *Keeping our words. The 1988 National Preservation Office competition*, London, The British Library, 1989.

Ogden, B. W., 'Determining conservation options at the University of California at Berkeley', in Merrill-Oldham, J. and Smith, M. (eds.), *The Library Preservation Program. Models, priorities, possibilities*, Chicago, Ill., American Library Association, 1985, 63 – 8.

Ogden, S., 'The impact of the Florence flood on library conservation in the United States of America', *Restaurator*, **3**, 1979, 1 – 36.

Palmer, R. E. (ed.), *Preserving the word* (Library Association Conference Proceedings, Harrogate, 1986), London, The Library Association, 1987.

Parker, T. A., *Study on integrated pest management for libraries and archives. A RAMP study*, Paris, Unesco (PGI-88/WS/20), 1988.

Parry, D., *Newsplan. Report of the Newsplan Project in the northern region, October 1987 – September 1988*, London, The British Library, 1989.

Pascoe, M. W., *Impact of environmental pollution on the preservation of archives and records: a RAMP study*, Paris, Unesco (PGI-88/WS/18), 1988.

Peacock, P. G., 'The selection of periodicals for binding', *Aslib proceedings*, **33**, 1981, 257 – 9.

Pickwoad, N., 'Conservation binding', in Ratcliffe, F. W., *Preservation policies and conservation in British libraries: Report of the Cambridge University Library Conservation Project*, London, The British Library (Library and Information Research Report, 25), 1984, 119 – 24.

Pollock, M., 'Surveying the collections', *Library conservation news*, **21**, October 1988, 4 – 6.

Price, R., 'Preserving the word: conservation in the Wellcome Institute Library', in National Preservation Office, *Conservation in crisis* (National Preservation Office, Seminar Papers, 1), London, The British Library, 1987, 49 – 55.

Priest, D. J., 'Paper and its problems', *Library review*, **36**, 1987, 164 – 73.

Ratcliffe, F. W., 'Education in preservation for librarians and archivists', in Palmer, R. E. (ed.), *Preserving the word* (Library Association Conference Proceedings, Harrogate, 1986), London, The Library Association, 1987, 95 – 105.

Ratcliffe, F. W., 'Preservation: a decade of progress', *Library review*, **36**, 1987, 228 – 36.

Ratcliffe, F. W., *Preservation policies and conservation in British libraries: Report of the Cambridge University Library Conservation Project*, London, The British Library (Library and Information Research Report, 25), 1984.

Rebsamen, W., 'Binding', *Library trends*, **30**, 1981 – 2, 225 – 39.

Reed, R., *Ancient skins, parchments and leathers*, London, Seminar Press, 1972.

Rees, E., 'Wales and the preservation problem', *Library conservation news*, **18**, January 1988, 1 – 3.

Rees, E., 'Wales and the preservation problem', in Palmer, R. E. (ed.), *Preserving the word* (Library Association Conference Proceedings, Harrogate, 1986), London, The Library Association, 1987, 29 – 32.

Roberts, M., 'The role of the librarian in the binding process', *Special libraries*, **62**, 1971, 413 – 20.

Roper, M., 'Policy for format conversion: choosing a format', in Smith, M. A. (ed.), *Preservation of library materials* (Conference held at the National Library of Austria, Vienna, 7 – 19 April 1986, sponsored by the Conference of Directors of National Libraries in co-operation with IFLA and Unesco), 2 vols, Munich, London, New York, Paris, K. G. Saur (IFLA Publications, 40, 41), 1987, vol. 1, 59 – 67.

Scott, M., 'Mass deacidification at the National Library of Canada', in Smith, M. A. (ed.), *Preservation of library materials* (Conference held at the National Library of Austria, Vienna, 7 – 19 April 1986, sponsored by the Conference of Directors of National Libraries in co-operation with IFLA and Unesco), 2 vols, Munich, London, New York, Paris, K. G. Saur (IFLA Publications, 40, 41), 1987, vol. 2, 134 – 6.

Silver, J. and Stickells, L., 'Preserving sound recordings at the British Library National Sound Archive', *Library conservation news*, **13**, October 1986, 1 – 3.

Smith, M. A., 'Care and handling of bound materials', in Smith, M. A. (ed.), *Preservation of library materials* (Conference held at the National Library of Austria, Vienna, 7 – 19 April 1986, sponsored by the Conference of Directors of National Libraries in co-operation with IFLA and Unesco), 2 vols, Munich, London, New York, Paris, K. G. Saur (IFLA Publications, 40, 41), 1987, vol. 2, 45 – 54.

Smith, M. A., 'The IFLA Core Program in Preservation and Conservation (PAC)', *IFLA journal* **12**, 1986, 305 – 6.

Smith, M. A. (ed.), *Preservation of library materials* (Conference held at the National Library of Austria, Vienna, 7 – 19 April 1986, sponsored by the Conference of Directors of National Libraries in co-operation with IFLA and Unesco), 2 vols, Munich, London, New York, Paris, K. G. Saur (IFLA Publications, 40, 41), 1987.

Sparks, P. G., 'Mass deacidification at the Library of Congress', in Smith, M. A. (ed.), *Preservation of library materials* (Conference held at the National

Library of Austria, Vienna, 7 – 19 April 1986, sponsored by the Conference of Directors of National Libraries in co-operation with IFLA and Unesco), 2 vols, Munich, London, New York, Paris, K. G. Saur (IFLA Publications, 40, 41), 1987, vol. 2, 137 – 40.

Stam, D. H., 'Collaborative collection development: progress, problems, and potential', *IFLA journal*, **12**, 1986, 9 – 19.

Stam, D. H., *National preservation planning in the United Kingdom: an American perspective*, London, The British Library (Research and Development Department Report, 5759), 1983.

Streit, S. A., 'Transfer of materials from general stacks to special collections', *Collection management*, **7**, 1985, 33 – 46.

Sturges, P., 'Policies and criteria for the archiving of electronic publishing', *Journal of librarianship*, **19**, 1987, 152 – 72.

Swartzburg, S. G. (ed.), *Conservation in the library. A handbook of use and care of traditional and nontraditional materials*, London, Aldwych Press, 1983.

Thomas, D., 'Conservation: new techniques and attitudes', *Archives*, **16**, 1983, 167 – 77.

Thomas D., *Study on control of security and storage of holdings: a RAMP study with guidelines*, Paris, Unesco (PGI-86/WS/23), 1987.

Thomas, D., 'Training conservation technicians: an archivist's view', in Ratcliffe, F. W., *Preservation policies and conservation in British libraries: Report of the Cambridge University Library Conservation Project*, London, The British Library (Library and Information Research Report, 25), 1984, 125 – 6.

Thompson, J. C., 'Mass deacidification: thoughts on the Cunha Report', *Restaurator*, **9**, 1988, 147 – 62.

Tregarthen Jenkin, I., *Disaster planning and preparedness: an outline disaster control plan*, London, The British Library (British Library Information Guides, 5), 1987.

Turner, J., 'Binding arbitration. A comparison of the durability of various hardback and paperback bindings', *Library Association record*, **88**, 1986, 233 – 5.

Turner, J. R., 'Teaching conservation', *Education for information*, **6**, 1988, 145 – 51.

Turner, M. L., 'Conservation in the Bodleian: a case study', in Ratcliffe, F. W., *Preservation policies and conservation in British libraries: Report of the Cambridge University Library Conservation Project*, London, The British Library (Library and Information Research Report, 25), 1984, 127 – 31.

Wächter, W., 'Mechanising restoration work – the Deutsche Bucherei, Leipzig, and its role as a regional centre for IFLA', *IFLA journal*, **12**, 1986, 307 – 9.

Walker, G., 'Advanced preservation planning at Yale', *Microform review*, **18**, 1989, 20 – 8.

Walker, G., 'Preserving the intellectual content of deteriorated library materials', in Morrow, C. C. (ed.), *The preservation challenge. A guide to conserving library materials*, White Plains, NY, Knowledge Industry Publications, 1983, 93 – 113.

Waters, P., 'The Florence flood of 1966 revisited', in Palmer, R. E. (ed.), *Preserving the word* (Library Association Conference Proceedings, Harrogate, 1986), London, The Library Association, 1987, 113 – 28.

Welsh, W. J., 'Experiments with optical disk technology at the Library of Congress', *IATUL proceedings*, **18**, 1986, 41 – 9.

Welsh, W. J., 'International cooperation in preservation of library materials', *Collection management*, **9**, 1987, 119 – 31.

White, S. B. and White, A. E., 'The computer: when tomorrow becomes yesterday', in Swartzburg, S. G. (ed.), *Conservation in the library. A handbook of use and care of traditional and nontraditional materials*, London, Aldwych Press, 1983, 205 – 19.

Williamson, H., *Methods of book design. The practice of an industrial craft*, 3rd ed., New Haven, Conn., Yale University Press, 1983.

Wilson, A., 'For this and future generations: managing the conflict between conservation and use', *Library review*, **31**, 1982, 163 – 72.

Wilson, A., *Library policy for preservation and conservation in the European Community. Principles, practices and the contribution of the new technology*, Munich, New York, London, Paris, K. G. Saur (CEC Publication EUR 11563), 1988.

Wood Lee, M., *Prevention and treatment of mold in library collections with an emphasis on tropical climates. A RAMP study*, Paris, Unesco (PGI-88/WS/9), 1988.

Index

film
  characteristics of 6 – 7, 38,
    41 – 2
  chemical constitution of 28 – 30
  colour 29
floppy discs 6 – 7, 30 – 1
Florence floods, 1966 3, 4
fold testing 67
France, preservation policies
    101 – 2
freeze-drying 71

Germany, preservation policies
    102 – 3
guard books 26

hard discs 30 – 1
heating systems 36, 63
humidity 38 – 42, 63

ICA 104
IFLA 104
information preservation 6, 56 – 7
insects 43 – 4
international activities 103 – 5

leather
  characteristics of 20 – 2
  manufacture of 20
  use in bookbindings 20 – 1
library binding 25
Library conservation news 100
Library of Congress 3, 6, 8, 51,
    98
lighting systems 42 – 3
light levels 42

Mellon Foundation 101
methyl magnesium carbonate
    process 6
mould growth 41

National Library of Scotland,
    Edinburgh 9, 51, 69
National Library of Wales,
    Aberystwyth 9

National Manuscripts Conservation
    Trust 101
National Preservation Advisory
    Committee 100
National Preservation Office
    (UK) 100, 101
National Register of Microform
    Masters 104

newspapers
  microfilming of 78 – 9
  preservation of 7, 76 – 9
Newsplan 101
New York Public Library 3, 4, 6

optical discs 30 – 1, 37

PAC Programme 104 – 5
PAC regional centres 104
paper
  acidic 4, 18 – 20, 66
  brittle 4, 5 – 6, 37, 97
  characteristics of 3, 14 – 20
  history of 14 – 15
  manufacture of 15 – 18
  repair of 5 – 7
paperbacks 80 – 1
parchment 20
perfect binding 26
periodicals 79 – 80
photographic studios 85 – 6
pH testing 66
pollution 44 – 5
preservation
  definition 2
  management aspects 4 – 5, 7,
    49 – 59, 76 – 94
  surveys for 64 – 7, 71 – 3
  techniques of 71 – 2
  training for 92 – 4
preservation surveys 3, 6, 8 – 10
public libraries 8, 50, 58 – 9

Ratcliffe Report 9, 99 – 101
rebacking 87 – 8

121